W9-CTO-873

"Korean Business Etiquette is a very easy, informative and useful read. It explains the origins and recent developments of the Korean business culture in an informed and insightful manner. It should be mandatory reading for foreign CEOs in Korea and any foreign businessperson conducting Commercial or Labor negotiations here."

— Joe Day, CEO of Market Entry Services and
Vice President of the EU Chamber of Commerce in Korea

"This is a wonderful, insightful book that you must read and study if you plan on having anything to do with the people of South Korea. Your chances of succeeding in Korea will be greatly enhanced by its profound cultural insights and practical advice."

— Steve McKinney, CEO McKinney Consulting, Inc.,Seoul

"If you are considering entering the Korean marketplace or working with Koreans, this book will show you what really makes them tick— and how to do business the Korean way. This work provides a focused mix of authoritative scholarship, practical insights and guidelines for foreigners working in Korea. It is "must reading" for anyone venturing into this complex but rewarding market."

— Martin H. Sours, Professor of International Studies,
The American Graduate School of International Management

Other books by Boyé Lafayette De Mente:

Asian Face Reading: Unlock the Secrets Hidden in the Human Face
Business Guide to Japan: Opening Doors...and Closing Deals
Chinese Etiquette & Ethics in Business
Chinese in Plain English
Discovering Cultural Japan: A Guide to Appreciating and
  Experiencing the Real Japan
Etiquette Guide to Japan: Know the Rules...that Make the Difference
Instant Japanese: Everything You Need in 100 Key Words
Japan's Cultural Code Words
Japanese Business Dictionary: English to Japanese
Japanese Etiquette & Ethics in Business
Japanese Influence on America: The Impact, Challenge and Opportunity
Japanese in Plain English
Japan Made Easy—All You Need to Know to Enjoy Japan
Kata: The Key to Understanding and Dealing with the Japanese
Korea's Business & Cultural Code Words
Korean in Plain English
Shopper's Guide to Japan
Survival Japanese: How to Communicate Without Fuss or Fear—Instantly!
The Chinese Have a Word for It: The Complete Guide to Chinese Thought
  and Culture
The Japanese Have a Word for It: The Complete Guide to Japanese
  Thought and Culture
Instant Chinese
Instant Korean
Survival Chinese
Survival Korean

KOREAN BUSINESS ETIQUETTE

The Cultural Values and Attitudes That Make Up the Korean Business Personality

Boyé Lafayette De Mente

TUTTLE PUBLISHING
Tokyo • Rutland, Vermont • Singapore

Published by Tuttle Publishing, an imprint of Periplus Editions (HK) Ltd, with editorial offices at 364 Innovationn Drive, North Clarendon, VT 05759 USA and 61 Tai Seng Avenue, #02-12, Singapore 534167.

LCC Card No. 2004303156

ISBN 978-0-8048-3582-4

Printed in Singapore

Distributed by:

North America, Latin America & Europe
Tuttle Publishing
364 Innovation Drive
North Clarendon, VT 05759-9436 USA
Tel: 1 (802) 773 8930,
Fax: 1 (802) 773 6993
Email: info@tuttlepublishing.com
www.tuttlepublishing.com

Japan
Tuttle Publishing
Yaekari Building, 3F
5-4-12 Osaki, Shinagawa-ku,
Tokyo 141-0032
Tel: (81) 3 5437 0171
Fax: (81) 3 5437 0755
Email: tuttle-sales@gol.com

Asia Pacific
Berkeley Books Pte Ltd
61 Tai Seng Avenue
#02-12, Singapore 534167
Tel: (65) 6280 1330,
Fax: (65) 6280 6290
Email: inquiries@periplus.com.sg
www.periplus.com

12 11 10 09 08   7 6 5 4 3

Contents

A Historical Profile

The Early Kingdoms

The Korean peninsula has been inhabited for at least 30,000 years and perhaps, tens of thousands of years longer. Prior to 1000 BC, family clans lived in villages, tilled the fields around them, hunted and fished. Their religion consisted of Shamanism, in which natural objects such as trees, rivers and rocks were believed to have spirits. (The same religion survives today, especially in rural areas.)

Korea's Bronze Age began around 1000 BC. It lasted for about a thousand years and was followed by an Iron Age which ended in approximately AD 935. In 350 BC, its first tribal league, Chosun, was at the apex of its power. It was centered in north Korea. Other tribal groups that existed on the Korean peninsula at that time included the Chinhan, Pyonhan and Mahan.

In 108 BC, China sent a large expeditionary force to Korea and established a kind of vassal relationship with the tribal leagues. These soon coalesced into three competing kingdoms—Silla (57 BC–AD 935), Paekche (18 BC–AD 600) and Koguryo (37 BC–AD 668).

By the first century AD, the people of the three Korean kingdoms had already developed a sophisticated lifestyle based on patterns long established in China. This development continued during the next several centuries, with Buddhism and Confucianism being added to their native religion of Shamanism.

The Korean kingdoms also adopted China's social and political systems, and divided the people into classes, with the royal families, elite government administrators and educators at the top. Besides this, the Chinese system of writing was also adopted. Those wishing to enter governmental service competed in annual examinations—another import from China.

In AD 668, the kingdom of Silla became supreme throughout the peninsula, and gave Korea its first golden age. When Silla was at its peak between AD 700 and 800, its capital city, Kyongju, had a population of over one million and was one of the most modern cities in the world. Many of Korea's greatest Buddhist temples were also built during this period. This too,was the period that saw the rise of unarmed martial arts.

The Silla dynasty gave way to the Koryo dynasty (from which modern Korea takes its name) in AD 935. The Koryo king gave Buddhism special status in the country in AD 950 and it played a dominant role in the history of the country until the fall of the dynasty in 1392. Confucianism, which is more of a social system than a religion, also permeated the Korean culture during the Koryo period and enjoyed its heyday during the next great dynasty.

The importance of Buddhism and Confucianism, both of which relied on written texts for their propagation, led to Korea's first printing press, which originally used wooden blocks and then began using movable metal type in AD 1234—a first in the world. Korea's famed celadon pottery was also developed during this period.

In the latter part of the 1200s, Genghis Khan and his Mongol hordes made Koryo a vassal state of China. King Kojong fled to the island of Kwangha, where he had all the Buddhist scriptures carved on 81,258 wooden blocks, an undertaking that required 16 years. (The blocks may be seen today at the Haein-Sa Mountain Temple.) The Mongol influence in Korea lasted for over 100 years.

The Last Dynasty

Korea's last dynasty (Choson or Yi) was founded in AD 1392, when General Song-Gye Yi (Yi is also written as Lee) seized power. Yi moved the capital to Seoul, its present location.

The Choson government adopted a new, extreme form of Confucianism as the foundation of both the government and society, dividing the people into classes and beginning the process of establishing a system of etiquette and ethics that was to prevail for the next 500 years and create the national character that continues to distinguish Koreans to this day.

The most famous of the Yi kings was Sejong, who ascended the throne in 1418. An enlightened and progressive ruler, Sejong established schools throughout the country where learned professors taught political science, history, medicine, geography and other subjects, including of course, Confucianism.

Sejong is personally credited with making significant technological advances in water clocks, the sundial, rain gauges and the lunar calendar. He was also responsible for setting up a team of scholars to specifically devise a purely Korean system of writing called *hangul* (hahn-guul) for the country's language.

Sejong's successors continued to expand the influence of the new and extreme form of Confucianism throughout the government and society. In 1471, these neo-Confucian principles were codified in the country's Great Administration Code and made the law of the land.

This newly enacted law officially established four distinct hereditary social classes. The elite *yangban*, made up of scholars and high ranking military officers, was designated the ruling class. Next came the *joong-in*, made up of professionals (doctors, lawyers, geographers, translators and middle-ranked military officers). Third in rank were the *sang-min*, which included artisans, craftsmen, fishermen, farmers who were ex-soldiers, and merchants.

The lowest class was made up of servants, butchers, entertainers, *kisaeng* girls, sorcerers, felons and slaves. The code also decreed that only direct lineal male members of the highest class (the *yangban*) were eligible to take the civil service examinations for government service, which had been held annually since the year AD 655. Part of the preparation for the civil service exams was learning some 20,000 Chinese characters (King Sejong's simplified *hangul* characters didn't count) and mastering the art of calligraphy.

This new Confucian state, which emphasized the past and with few exceptions, discouraged change or innovation of any kind, kept Korea at a virtual standstill for the next 400 years.

During the more than 500 years of the Choson dynasty, several generations usually lived in a family compound—the men in the front and the women in the back. Boys and girls were separated at the age of seven, at which time boys started school while girls were kept at home—and in lower-class families, acted as servants to the male members of the family. When sons married, they set up housekeeping in their family compound.

Men were free to come and go as they pleased, but women were virtually slaves. Upper-class women were prohibited from leaving their compounds during the day, and could go out at night for brief periods only with the permission of their husbands. In Seoul, the hour at which the women could leave their homes and go outside was noted by the ringing of a great bell, which also sounded when they were to be back home.

Because of this strictly enforced edict, many women lived all their lives without seeing Seoul during daylight hours. Men could divorce their wives at any time for any one of seven "sins," among which were talking too much, not pleasing their mothers-in-law and failure to bear sons. This social system prevailed in Korea until well into the 20th century, and was responsible for fashioning what is now often referred to as the traditional Korean character.

Contact with Japan

Prior to the establishment of the Choson dynasty in 1392, Korea's relations with Japan had mostly been friendly. In fact, Korea, along with China, had been the wellspring for much of Japanese civilization from around 350 AD. But in the mid-1400s, Japanese pirates began raiding the Korean coastal areas, and thereafter, relations between the two countries started to deteriorate.

In 1592, Japan's Hideyoshi Toyotomi, who had become the supreme military power in Japan after a long period of clan warfare, sent a huge army to Korea, determined to conquer the peninsula and then proceed on to invade China—apparently to extract revenge from the Chinese for their role in the attempted invasions of Japan by Genghis Khan and his Mongol hordes in 1274 and 1281.

However, the first Japanese invasion ships to approach Korea were defeated by Korea's famed Admiral Sun-Shin Yi, whose ironclad warships—the world's first—caught the Japanese by surprise. But the large Japanese army of skilled and experienced warriors was not to be denied. They eventually established a beachhead, then began a systematic campaign of laying waste to the country and butchering everyone who opposed them. They sliced the ears off thousands of their victims, pickled them and sent them back to Japan as evidence of their success.

The Japanese occupied large portions of Korea and settled in for a long campaign. Among them was a Spanish Catholic priest and first recorded Westerner to set foot in Korea, who began preaching Christianity to Koreans in the conquered areas.

Before the Japanese army could complete the subjugation of Korea, however, Hideyoshi Toyotomi became ill. Fearful that his newly established military control of Japan might be threatened, he had the army recalled from Korea. He died before they could reach Japan and prevent his fears from coming true.

The death and destruction wrought on Korea by the Japanese soured Koreans on having any kind of foreign relations. The country was sealed off to the outside world and was known as "The Hermit Kingdom" for almost 300 years. Ironically, it was also Japan that later pried the Hermit Kingdom open, then brought its downfall.

In 1876, a Japanese ship appeared off the coast of southern Korea and was fired on by shore batteries. When the ship's crew returned to Japan and reported the incident, the highly militant Japanese mounted a crushing attack against the inexperienced and primitively armed Korean defense forces, and once again established a beachhead on Korean soil.

Colonization by Japan

Japan demanded that Korea renounce its isolationist policy and open its ports to Japanese naval and merchant ships (in an almost exact reenactment of their own experiences—minus the invasion—with the US in the 1850s). Six years later, Korea extended the same rights to the US, and shortly thereafter, to other nations as well.

From this time, Japan rapidly extended its influence in Korea, resulting in a breakdown of its relations with China and Russia. Following a successful war against China in 1895 and against Russia in 1904 and 1905, Japan began turning Korea into a colony, taking over its government and all major industries.

In 1910, Japan formally ended the Choson dynasty by making Korea a part of the Japanese empire. The Japanese occupation forces immediately began a brutal program aimed at Japanizing the Koreans by outlawing their language and many of their cultural practices, and forcing them to adopt Japanese names.

Japan's control of Korea continued until the end of World War II in 1945, when it was defeated by the US and its allies. Unfortunately, the US agreed to allow Russia to administer the portion of Korea north of the 38th parallel until a Korean government could be established to replace the defeated Japanese. The Russians immediately established a communist regime in northern Korea and refused all entreaties to reunite the country thereafter.

Elections were held in South Korea in 1948. Syngman Rhee, a patriot who had long been in exile in Hawaii, was elected president. In the meantime, the USSR installed Il-Sung Kim, a dedicated communist who had been indoctrinated in the Soviet Union, as president of North Korea. After five years of communist indoctrination, North Korean troops invaded South Korea in June 1950, believing that the only way to reunite the country was to drive the Americans out of South Korea.

US and UN troops soon pushed the invading North Koreans back to the Yalu River, and the war seemed to be over. China then joined the fighting on the side of North Korea. US and UN forces suffered heavy losses and were driven southward to the vicinity of Pusan.

General Douglas MacArthur, Supreme Commander of the Allied Powers occupying Japan at that time, led the US forces in a counterattack through the port of Inchon west of Seoul on the Yellow Sea side of the peninsula. The move outflanked the Chinese and North Koreans and drove them back to the 38th parallel, where the war became stalemated as the result of a political decision by the US government. A cease-fire was then called and in July 1953, an armistice agreement was signed, establishing a two-kilometer demilitarized zone along the 38th parallel and setting up the framework for peace talks between the North and South.

More than half a century later, the talks are still going on and the country is still divided. Families that were torn apart have not seen each other since 1950. And like the infamous Communist Wall in Berlin, the demilitarized zone and the peace talk site at Panmunjom have become tourist attractions.

The Korean War and Its Aftermath

The Korean War (1950–1953) brought new death and destruction to South Koreans on a massive scale. But the suffering of the Korean people was not over. The government under Syngman Rhee was rife with corruption and the abuse of power. Student uprisings finally forced Rhee to retire in 1960.

With Rhee gone, Myun J. Chang took over as president but in May 1961, a bloodless coup led by General Chung-Hee Pak cut short his administration.

For the next eight years, ex-general Pak gave South Korea harsh but efficient rule, instituting many reforms and inaugurating the first of a series of five-year plans that created an economic miracle. Pak was assassinated in October 1979. Kyu-Hah Choi served as president for two months and was replaced on December 12 1979 by Doo-Hwan Chun, under whose strict military-style leadership the economic miracle of the Republic of South Korea continued to unfold.

In early 1987, disenchantment with the militaristic regime of ex-General Doo-Hwan Chun reached a boiling point. University students once again took to the streets, bringing on a series of increasingly violent confrontations with the national police and armed forces. Finally, Tae-Woo Roh, newly appointed chairman of the ruling Democratic Justice Party and Chun's hand-picked successor, abruptly capitulated to the demands of the students and the main opposition parties, and announced in late June that the constitution would be revised and a democratic form of government adopted.

It is against this backdrop of Shamanism, Buddhism, Confucianism, a strict hierarchal society and decades of suffering and anguish at the hands of foreign powers, along with internal political strife, that one must view present-day Korea and its people.

The American Chamber of Commerce (AmCham) in Korea—the primary source of information and guidance on the mechanics of doing business in Korea—notes that the Korean business environment has undergone enormous changes since the late 1990s, with a huge number of regulations amended or wiped off the books altogether, and the process continues. AmCham adds that Korea is more open to and welcoming of international business than it has ever been in the past.

Korea, continues AmCham, is a highly strategic market in terms of its geographic location and economic power, offering a low-cost, highly educated workforce with a work ethic that propelled the country from a virtual wasteland to one of the world's largest economies in just one short generation.

Amcham reminds foreign businesspeople that the cultural aspect of doing business in Korea takes precedence over virtually all other considerations and that while Koreans often make exceptions for foreigners, there are many customs and norms the expatriate businessperson encounters daily that cannot be ignored.

Surprising perhaps to newcomers in the field of international business, expatriate managers in Korea (as in other foreign countries) generally end up having more problems with their head offices than they do in their local business relationships—mostly because head office personnel are unable to appreciate the imperatives of the Korean way of doing things, and the need to adapt and compromise.

INTRODUCTION

The "Force" is with Them!

From the beginning of their history, the common people of Korea lived under authoritarian-type regimes that generally prevented them from thinking and behaving as individuals, and dramatically limited the choices they had in how and where they lived. With the introduction of Confucianism into Korea over 2,000 years ago, restrictions on individual thought and behavior gradually became more onerous. When the Choson dynasty was established in 1392, it adopted an even more restrictive form of neo-Confucianism that totally controlled the lives of the people, requiring them to repress virtually all of the emotions, spirit, intellect and ambitions that are inherent in human beings.

In brief, the form of Confucianism adopted by the new Choson dynasty in 1392 and in the decades that followed emphasized what has been called a "father culture." It gave fathers absolute authority over their families, made ancestor worship the primary religion and required unquestioned obedience to fathers, father figures and government officials, combined with unqualified respect for seniors and elders in general.

This system, which lasted until 1945, built up in the psyche of Koreans a powerful "force" that Korean sociologists refer to as *han* (hahn) or unrequited resentments—a force that could be equated to the pressure that builds up in a pot of boiling water that is kept so tightly covered that no steam can escape.

The sociologists go on to say that during Korea's long feudal era there were many kinds of *han*—the *han* of political abuse, the *han* of sexual abuse, the *han* of poverty, the *han* of wartime suffering, the *han* of class immobility and so on—all the institutionalized limitations on the freedom to be individuals and the hardships Koreans had to endure over the ages.

Described another way, *han* refers to the buildup of unrequited yearnings that were created by oppressive religious and political systems; by life in a society in which most of the normal human drives were subverted or totally denied; by a state of constant fear of offending someone; and by intense and permanent feelings of frustration, repressed anger, regret, remorse, grief, deprivation and helplessness.

By law and by custom, premodern Korea's political and social systems kept the people sealed up in cages that prevented them from developing even a fraction of their potential. They became like steel springs that were pressed nearly flat, with few approved ways to release their energy, curiosity or creativity.

Korean poetry abounds because it was one of the few ways that the people could express themselves without breaking any of the social customs or laws, and it is replete with expressions of *han*—deep feelings of sadness, frustration and resentment.

About the only initiative that was allowed during the long Choson dynasty was that sponsored by a few of the reigning Choson kings, the greatest of which was King Sejong. He sponsored a large group of scholars and scientists at a research institute and personally oversaw the creation of a script for writing the Korean language, which up to that time had been written using Chinese characters, and which is now regarded as one of the simplest, clearest and most scientific of all writing systems.

There are 10 vowels and 14 consonants in the alphabet that are combined to form the numerous syllables that make up individual words. [And unlike the Chinese characters, which takes years to master, Korea's *hangul* alphabet can be learned in a day or so.]

As long as the power of Korea's feudal dynasties was sufficient to keep the people in a vice that controlled virtually every thought and action, they appeared to be passive and content. But when this power weakened as it did periodically, they would explode in violence.

Nothing angered, frustrated and humiliated the proud Koreans more, or added more to their *han* burden, than the occupation and colonization of their country by Japan in 1910.

When Koreans were finally freed in 1945 from the compression chamber in which they had existed for so long, they turned their unleashed ambition, creativity and energy into building an economic and social super power in one generation.

Foreigners dealing with Koreans today should be aware of the powerful feelings of *han* that continue to drive them. The extraordinary energy they bring to their education, to their work and their determination to succeed is still fueled by the great psychic bang that occurred when they were finally freed from the physical and mental cage they had lived in for so long.

Despite fundamental changes in the Korean mindset and behavior since the last half of the 20th century, the teachings of Confucius, the ancient Chinese sage, remain the bedrock of Korean culture, and must be taken into account in virtually all dealings with Koreans, including those who have become partially Westernized.

Young Koreans may dress and generally act like Americans for example, but the prevailing social system today still includes many facets of traditional Confucianism—close-knit families, a powerful compulsion to achieve the highest possible education, mutual responsibility for the welfare of the family and relatives, and ongoing respect for seniors.

Ethnically, Koreans belong to the Mongolian race, but their language and culture differ fundamentally from that of the Chinese, Japanese and Mongolians. All Koreans speak the same language with only minor regional variations. As in all societies, especially ancient ones, the Korean language is both the primary reservoir of the traditional culture and the vehicle that sustains it and passes it on from one generation to the next. Key words in the language serve as windows to the heart, soul and mindset of the people.

I suggest that no one can fully understand Koreans or fully appreciate Korean culture without being relatively fluent in the Korean language. The Korean national character and pattern of thinking is directly related to the language, not only in its use as a routine communications medium, but in all of the nuances of the culture.

Since mastering the Korean language and all of its cultural components is a major challenge—one that foreign businesspeople stationed in Korea did not begin to take seriously until the 1990s—the best preliminary option is to become familiar with key words that provide insight into the heart and soul of Koreans.

In fact, one cannot function properly in Korean society today without knowing the right words to use for specific occasions, and precisely how to use them. The choice in vocabulary that the speaker has to make covers virtually every aspect of society—gender, age, position, class, the circumstances of the moment and so on.

To paraphrase one Korean language authority: The Korean language is designed to reveal and maintain the social status of speakers. In any conversation who is the inferior and who is the superior quickly becomes obvious. Because Koreans have become so sensitized to language, it is extremely important for people to use humble and modest expressions to avoid offending anyone.

This authority adds that Koreans are "slaves" to the demands of language etiquette. This circumstance is changing, however, albeit slowly with the times.

Korean language authorities also note that it ranges from difficult to impossible to speak logically in Korean because the language is designed to be vague and lacks sufficient abstract terms. Because of this, a great deal of the communication between Koreans is based on intuition, "reading" the other person's mind and verbal cues, rather than on precise verbalization.

In addition to a special form of polite or honorific speech that is used when addressing superiors in a variety of formal situations, there are six recognized Korean dialects in different areas of the country, plus a form of Korean that is known as "crude language," which is used by people who are generally outside the pale of normal society.

Work as Religion

One of the legacies of Confucianism that played an extraordinarily positive role in the emergence of Korea as one of the world's leading economic powers is the convergence of many of the teachings of Confucius into a work ethic and success drive that is astounding.

In fact, modern-day Koreans have converted Confucianism, with much of its discipline and group consciousness, into a work cult. Once they were free to better themselves, getting an education and getting ahead became the primary goals in their lives, and they continue to pursue these goals with religious fervor.

The Lust for Power

Another aspect of modern-day Korean culture that impacts on the prevailing ethics is a passion for success and *him* (heem), or power, that is so common that it can aptly be described as a Korean trait. This syndrome is a legacy of the long centuries when all power was in the hands of the upper elite class that administered the affairs of the country.

When the government system that had divided the country into social classes and relegated all authority and power to the upper-class—and to fathers in all classes—was abolished, it was a true social, economic and political emancipation for the bulk of the population.

For the first time in the history of the Koreans, everyone was free to pursue success and power to whatever degree they wanted and were capable of achieving. They had never had the power to control their lives, and the energy released by this newly achieved freedom provided a dynamism and creativity that had never before existed in the country.

The passion for *him*, combined with a fierce pride in their country, drove the Koreans to get the best possible education, the best possible job, and to work with uncommon diligence and energy.

The resulting drive for power not only became one of the primary factors in the national character of Koreans—it became the foundation for the country's subsequent rise to economic prominence.

Fighting at the Drop of a Hat

History books on Korea have made a big "to do" about an ancient Chinese description of the country as "The Land of Morning Calm." This line was written by a Chinese observer who was impressed with the utter calmness of the Korean countryside bathed in the early morning light (with fog covering the tops of nearby hills).

In more recent centuries, early Western visitors to Korea repeatedly commented on the calmness of the people, and its lack of violence. These commentators did not bother to add that Koreans were typically calm and passive because the culture, the society and the government did not sanction any other kind of behavior, and used draconian measures to ensure passivity and calmness.

The fact is, individual Koreans—both men and women—often exploded into violence of one kind or another when they were no longer able to keep their repressed emotions and desires bottled up. With the men, this explosion of violence usually took the form of drinking to excess and then fighting.

In fact, in the early days of the Choson Dynasty (1392–1910), public *chontu* (chohn-tuu), or fights, were so common among men that the government issued an edict that men would wear heavy ceramic hats rather than hats made of horsehair, and if they got into a brawl and their hat fell off they would be severely punished.

The volume of violence in Korea diminished dramatically for a number of decades thereafter. However, the heavy ceramic hats were so inconvenient that the government gradually became lax in enforcing the edict, and it finally withered away. [It seems logical that the common Western saying "fight at the drop of a hat" may have actually originated in Korea!]

When Japan occupied Korea in 1910, a Japanese military man wrote that Korean men were more interested in singing and poetry than in fighting. (Korea had an elite class of professional warriors long before Japan had its samurai, but the Korean warriors spent most of their time performing arts, rather than fighting.)

In reality, large numbers of Koreans resisted the Japanese occupation, hiding out in the mountains and fighting as guerillas. Others, forced to work for the Japanese, did all they could to sabotage the efforts of the Japanese to eliminate Korean culture.

But centuries of oppression under Confucian and Japanese regimes did not destroy the spirit of Koreans and once they were free, their spirits soared. Today, typical Koreans will, in fact, fight at the drop of a hat, to defend their face, their honor and their country.

The Legacy of Enforced Harmony

The first reference to Korea apparently appeared in a Chinese document written some 4,000 years ago. It described the people living on the Korean peninsula as being peaceful in their demeanor, with precise rules of etiquette that attested to the importance of *hwa* (whah), or harmony, in their society.

The culture of the Koreans at that time revolved around shamanistic beliefs that controlled their daily behavior, from interpersonal relationships between the sexes and the obligations of the people to superiors, to their agricultural activities. Some 2,000 years later, a dramatic event occurred.

In 108 BC, China, with its vastly superior civilization, invaded and virtually colonized the Korean peninsula. The Chinese overlords quickly introduced Koreans to their arts and crafts as well as to Buddhism and Confucianism, both of which were to have a fundamental influence on life in Korea.

Within a few generations, Buddhism had replaced many of the shamanistic rituals and customs of the Koreans and become the dominant religion on the peninsula. But as the centuries went by, organized Buddhism became so corrupt that it threatened the survival of the kingdoms and resulted in a bloody rebellion against the huge number of militant priests and their fortified monasteries.

With the power of the Buddhists broken, the winners of the rebellion established a new government based on Confucian principles. In 1392, the founders of the Choson dynasty (which endured until 1910), made a new and extremely rigid form of Confucianism the basis for a new set of laws that prescribed every aspect of etiquette and ethics of Korean life.

The rigid social system created by the Choson Court was designed to ensure absolute *hwa* in society—something with which the Koreans were already familiar, but in this case the laws were among the most repressive ever imposed on any group of people.

This social system prevailed in Korea until near the end of the 19th century. By this time, the ruling family and its ministers had become as corrupt as the ancient Buddhist priests, begun to lose control of the country, and had come under the influence of the Japanese, Russians and Europeans. In 1910, Japan took the extraordinary step of occupying and annexing the country, turning it into a province administered by the Japanese military.

Korea was freed from Japanese occupation in 1945, but the Confucian-based lifestyle of the vast majority of Koreans did not really begin to change until the 1950s and 60s. Even today, the influence of over 500 years of programming in Confucian etiquette and ethics is still present in Korean culture, and cannot be escaped or ignored.

Hwa is still the ideal in Korean society, but this does not mean the universal kind of emotional, spiritual, intellectual and physical harmony that the term connotes in English. It means Korean-style harmony, the kind that results from obeying all the dictates of the etiquette and ethics now prevailing in Korean society—etiquette and ethics that have their roots in Confucianism.

While it is true that Korea's younger generations have sloughed off most of the heavier cultural chains that bound their parents and ancestors, enough of the traditional Confucian attitudes and behavior remains to give present-day Korean culture a flavor of its own that is generally different enough from Western values and behavior so that they do not naturally mesh, making it necessary for the two sides to compromise in order to communicate effectively and work together.

The Clans Are Alive and Well

While foreign businesspeople might think that Korea's traditional clan system is ancient history and not something that they need to concern themselves about, this is not always the case in reality.

Like most ancient nations, Korea began as a collection of clans that gradually coalesced into tribal states and finally, unified kingdoms. But in the case of Korea, the original chok (choak), or clans, did not disappear over time. They survived into modern times since the influence of Shamanism, Confucianism and Buddhism worked against radical changes in society, and contributed to virtually all positions of authority in a clan being monopolized by the leading family—thus ensuring that the primary goal of each clan was that of its own survival within the existing kingdoms.

There are said to be 39 "root" clans in Korea, but more than 2,000 years ago, most of the peninsula was controlled by about a dozen clans. The two largest of the clans were the Kim and Yi (also spelled as Lee and Rhee). Today the Kim family has 32 clan branches and accounts for some one-quarter of the population of the country. The Lee family has five branches.

The Kims and Lees have remained the most prominent family clans since ancient times and still today, their numerous members dominate much of the economy, the politics, education and society in general. The family registers of these two clans go back 2,500 years.

While anti-discrimination laws are in place and discrimination may be denied, a person's clan affiliations and place of birth are important factors in education and employment in Korea—just as regional and racial factors still play a role in the lives of Americans.

Foreign employers in Korea should be aware of the subtleties involved in "mixing" workers from different clans, and take steps to prevent friction from developing.

The Problem of Names

One of the most unusual aspects of Korean society created by the prominence of a small number of clans over the centuries and one that also plays a vital role in business as well as all other areas of society, is names—people's names. Altogether there are only about 300 *song* (song), or family names, in Korea. The four largest and most influential of the family clans were—and still are—Kim, Pak, Lee and Choi.

Other major family clans included Choe, Chung, Kang, Cho, Yun, Chang (Jang) and Rim. Today, approximately half of all Koreans are named Kim, Lee or Pak. The other eight names account for another 15 percent of the population.

Many of the 300 or so family names in Korea are off-shoots of the founding families. Immigrants from China and Mongolia brought in some of the other names.

This name situation is said to stem from the fact that the names of the families that gave birth to the Korean population became imbued with a sacred quality that was assiduously maintained from one generation to the next. Confucianism incorporated the concept of revering one's ancestors, which further encouraged the maintenance of the family name and negated any inclination to adopt a new surname that would have no history and no honor.

It has also long been the custom for each Korean to have two given names—one a personal name and the other a generational name—chosen by the parents, grandparents or an onomancer (name-giver). A male generational name is given to the first son born in a family and a female generational name is given to the first daughter. Thereafter, all additional sons and daughters in the family are given the same male or female generational names.

As the family branches out over the generations, the generational names are continued in the male and female lines over three generations and then replaced by new ones, so that eventually people who are very distantly related may have a common generational name that goes back to a remote ancestor.

Because of the special and almost mystical role that names played in traditional Korean society, people were very sensitive about their names and there were numerous taboos about using them. In earlier times, many Koreans were so sensitive about their personal names that they did not like to hear other people say them aloud.

Still today, a great deal of thought goes into the selection of both personal and generational names, and it is common for parents to seek the help of professional name-givers. The object is to select a name that fits the child on the basis of the time it was born and the parents' expectations for the child.

Among Koreans, only family members and close friends address each other by their first names. Foreigners should not address new Korean contacts by their first names until a proper relationship has been established, and even then, only if their age, social and professional status are roughly equal—this reminder especially applies to Americans who are culturally programmed to equate the use of first names with equality and sincerity. Young people, including those in positions of authority, should not address older people by their first names.

Korean women do not change their names when they marry. They may be called by their maiden name, by the title of *puin* (puu-een) or *ojumoni* (oh-juu-moe-nee), meaning "wife," or "the wife of Mr. Lee," etc.

To get around the extraordinary problem created by the fact that every other Korean is either Kim, Lee, Pak or Choi, Koreans use titles connected with their profession, place of work and rank. In companies where there are dozens to hundreds of Lees, Kims, Paks and Chois who are all mangers, individuals are usually identified by their titles, along with their sections or divisions. If there are two or more "Manager Lee" in one section, they may be referred to as "Manager Lee of Production No. 1"; "Manager Lee of Production No. 2"; and so on.

"Names are indeed a horrendous problem," noted longtime Seoul resident Carole Alexander. "In one department [of the Westin Chosun Hotel] we had two Lees. We called one 'Senior Lee' and the other one 'Baby Lee.'" On the personal side, Koreans also use the areas where they live to identify each other.

Many of the most common names in Korea may be spelled two or three different ways. Some of the syllables making up the Korean language are also pronounced differently by many people, making the names sound different, especially to foreign ears that are not totally sensitized to the variations in the language.

This name situation creates special problems for newly arrived foreigners in Korea who try to telephone people they have recently met. Not being aware of the seriousness of the situation, they frequently fail to get or remember the titles and sections or departments of the people concerned, and are therefore unable to identify which Lee, Choi, Pak or Kim they want to talk to.

Koreans who have been educated abroad or have had substantial experience with Westerners in Korea have become accustomed to foreigners calling them Mr., Mrs. or Miss, and it is becoming more commonplace for them to also use these Western titles when addressing one another, especially when they do not know an individual's proper Korean title.

It is very important for foreign travelers and businesspeople visiting Korea to carefully write down the full name, title (if any) and company section of all Koreans whom they might want to call or meet again. On a personal level, it is also wise to get their home addresses and often their position in the family (first or second son or daughter, etc.). The name problem is one of the primary reasons why name cards are so important in doing business in Korea.

Until recent years, traditional-minded Koreans were extraordinarily sensitive about the use of first names. Before they could make a decision to use a foreign first name for example, they often had family meetings and discussed the matter endlessly, with a seriousness that astounds the uninitiated foreigner.

Said one veteran foreign businessperson in Seoul: "We had one man who worked for us for 15 years, and was known by everyone as 'Ted.' I met his daughter one day and was amazed to discover that she did not know her father had a foreign nickname."

Commented another foreign businessperson: "In my 17 years in Korea, I have been able to develop close, first-name relationships with only five Koreans. When I first arrived here, the US ambassador advised me that it would take me one year to get to know a Korean, two years before they would accept me (if I didn't make any terrible mistakes) and three years before I would be able to get any work done.

"The ambassador's timetable proved to be painfully accurate. US companies that assign managers here for only two or three years are wasting time and money. Friendship and trust must be built up on both sides, and if it is solid it will last a lifetime. Once you have established this kind of relationship with Koreans, they will never forget you and will do everything they can to maintain the relationship."

Personal names are one of the great inventions of humanity and family names are now so important to life in communities that it is hard to imagine living in a society in which the vast majority of people do not have family names. But that was the case in Korea. Men in the commoner class were not allowed to have family names until near the end of the 19th century and females in the same class were not granted the right until 1909.

A growing number of men, especially among those involved in international business of any kind, choose to go by the initial letters of their given names to make it easier for foreigners to understand and use. Chong-Chill Kim becomes C. C. Kim. Other families that have become international in their lifestyle dispense with the generational name altogether.

Another variation in the presentation of given and generational names that has been adopted by some English language news publications in Korea is to connect the two names with a hyphen, and begin the generational name with a small letter instead of a capital, i.e. Chong-chill.

The small number of family names in Korea causes identity problems among Koreans themselves, so it is easy to image how much more difficult it can be for foreigners to keep the Kims, Lees and Paks (or Parks) straight. In personal situations, it is common to use the district they live in, or their actual address, to help identify individuals. And it is sometimes necessary to use the family birth rank (first son, second son, etc.) to identify someone.

Foreign businesspeople visiting Korea or having Korean guests should, of course, make sure they get the name cards of individuals they meet and if there is not enough information on the cards to distinguish them, ask for more and write it down on the back of the card. (Not too long ago, name cards were held in such high esteem that it was considered bad form to write on them, but this cultural taboo is fading away.)

Because of the serious problem of distinguishing between so many people with the same last name in Korea, it is becoming more common for the Koreans to adopt *pyolmyong* (pyole-m'yong), or nicknames. Once you become acquainted with someone, it is appropriate to ask if they have a nickname.

It is also still the rule for Koreans to use *tojang* (toe-jahng), or name seals, in lieu of signing their names on ordinary letters or documents. Seals that are used for stamping official documents are known as *ingan* (een-gahn) and must be registered with the local authorities.

CHAPTER ONE

The Basis of Korean Etiquette and Ethics

The basic conduct and character of Koreans remains founded in the principles and teachings of the neo, all-encompassing form of Confucianism that was officially adopted by the Yi (now usually spelled as Lee) or Choson dynasty, which ruled the country from 1392 to 1910. The primary precepts of this neo-Confucianism were:

1. Total loyalty to a hierarchal structure of authority. This includes the parents, family, clan, community, and king or nation.

2. Duty to the parents, incorporating loyalty, love and gratitude, especially to the mother, who was portrayed (and usually was) a symbol of virtue, unselfishness and sacrifice.

3. Strict order and a minutely defined form of conduct between children and adults. Children are conditioned to pay absolute respect to their grandparents and parents (in that order), to obey them totally, and to demonstrate only the most respectful behavior toward them, including the use of respectful language, bowing and speaking only when spoken to. This extreme conditioning explains, of course, the respect present-day Koreans still have for older people, teachers and government officials. (No doubt in compensation for these strict rules of etiquette and conduct demanded of all young people in Korea, the very young were allowed to run free, almost without any discipline in the rest of their behavior, until they were about ten years old.)

4. Separation of the husband and wife. Men and women in Confucian Korea lived almost totally in separate spheres. Men lived in the front of the compound; their wives in the back. Men concerned themselves with outside affairs and the overall running of the family compound; women performed all of the housekeeping functions and the raising of the children, with absolutely no crossing over. Boys were sent to school to learn to read and write; girls were taught domestic skills at home.

5. Trust between friends. This was upheld as a prime virtue and was strongly emphasized as a vital part of the overall fabric of the society on a community level.

While the Confucian culture of Korea during the Choson era was responsible for one of the most peaceful and orderly societies that ever existed, there was also a downside to its extreme curtailment of the natural curiosity, creativity and individuality of human beings. Both Korean and foreign observers commenting on Korea's Confucian society in the early part of the 20th century noted that the narrow constrictions of the social system, suppressing as it did many of the natural impulses of the people, resulted in their being extremely emotional and hot-tempered, and inclined toward outbursts of rage, jealousy, cruelty and violence.

The social, political and educational systems in feudal Korea also negated the development of abstract, metaphysical and rational reasoning. This resulted in irrational behavior when the people were confronted with any situation outside of their highly structured lifestyle. The Confucian teachings and lifestyle also prevented the development of a separate sense of responsibility and ability to self-reflect on moral issues.

Dr. Kyong-Dong Kim, Professor and Director of the Social Science Institute in Seoul National University, has come up with a long list of cultural characteristics of the Koreans that might be categorized as the "isms of Korea." These include:

Authoritarianism—Emphasizing a superior-subordinate relationship between parents and children, the old and the young, male and female, and upper and lower social classes and ranks.

Collectivism—A strong inclination to look at and react to everything in terms of "familyism," with the accompanying inability to quickly and easily distinguish between what is private and what is public.

Connectionism—The deeply rooted habit of establishing all social and business relationships on personal connections (instead of more abstract factors such as mutual interests or mutual activities).

Conservatism—A continuing belief in the value of traditional ways and a tendency to be traditional in behavior.

Exclusivism—A strong tendency to form exclusive groups or factions centered on personal relations such as family, school, birthplace and community, which leads in turn to favoritism and nepotism.

Fatalism—Acceptance of things they think cannot be changed, such as abuse by politicians or browbeating by superiors, which leads to submissiveness and feelings of inferiority to outside authorities or power.

Secularism—A strong emphasis on worldly accomplishments, on working harder than anyone else, on producing more than anyone else and on building things bigger and better than anyone else.

Etiquette vs. Ethics

In premodern Korea, as in all Confucian-oriented cultures of Asia, a minutely structured social system and a precisely scripted etiquette took the place of ethics based on principles of right and wrong.

Koreans were ethical and moral if they conducted themselves according to the rules of conduct established by the government—rules that were based on sustaining a society that was hierarchically divided by gender and class, and ruled over by an elite upper class.

In this environment, relationships between people were absolutely controlled by an individual's gender and place in the inferior-superior and vertically arranged society. There was virtually no social intercourse between classes, and the elite, hereditary upper class reigned supreme.

Koreans also typically ignored those with whom they had no relationship, because to do otherwise would require establishing a connection that resulted in a variety of social obligations. This system dramatically limited the dynamics of Korean society as a whole—combined with the Confucian concept of worshipping ancestors and looking back instead of forward—was the reason why the country stagnated socially, politically and economically, until its encounter with Japan and the West at the end of the 19th century.

What all this means today insofar as business is concerned is the fact that *kongson* (kohng-sohn), or Korean-style courtesy, often takes precedence over Western concepts of ethical behavior. And this can be even more disconcerting to Westerners because the courtesy that Koreans exhibit toward others generally depends upon a number of factors—age, gender, position, social class and any existing relationship, etc.—and is not a universal thing.

Fortunately, as far as Koreans are concerned, foreigners are "cultural free"—meaning they are not bound by the rules of Korean etiquette and all the obligations involved—so Koreans have no qualms about meeting and interacting with them, and many in fact, aggressively seek relationships with foreigners for economic as well as social reasons.

The Perils of Using Logic

It is generally accepted that the foundation of Western thought is based on logical and rational reasoning—although this is not always obvious or real in the history of the West. Koreans on the other hand, were traditionally steeped in Confucian principles that gave precedence to an enforced social harmony that generally ignored both *nolli* (nohl-lee), or logic, and rationality insofar as natural human instincts and aspirations were concerned.

Koreans were conditioned to suppress their emotions, to eschew individualistic and independent thinking and behavior, and to scrupulously obey the etiquette and group orientation prescribed by Confucianism and interpreted by their authoritarian governments.

In this environment, the use of logic and rational thinking was taboo, except in special situations created and controlled by the authorities on different levels. Korean sociologist Chae-Sok Choe says that the traditional conditioning of Koreans in a formalistic, ritualistic social system made them incapable of rational thought and behavior.

Industrialization has its own mandates that demand logical and rational behavior, and the modernization of Korea has dramatically weakened the hold that Confucianism had on its culture. Koreans are no longer mired up to their necks in a social system based on illogic and irrationality, but most have not yet sloughed off the influence of centuries of intensive brainwashing that programmed them to regard much of the logic and rational thinking of the West as antisocial.

Westerners who present their arguments and cases to Koreans in a strictly logical manner with facts, figures and projections, almost always encounter some degree of resistance. In some instances, the resistance may be total. Still today, many Koreans regard people who always think and behave in a logical manner as disruptive rather than constructive, with extreme cases being looked upon as antihuman.

One of the most common complaints that Koreans have about Westerners—Americans in particular—is that their logical stance makes them inflexible and therefore hard to deal with. They also add that American businesspeople, diplomats and politicians talk too much, repeat themselves too often, and little by little weaken their own arguments in an effort to get agreements.

The Americans, they add, repeatedly use the terms "fair" and "just" in their arguments and presentations, without being aware that what is fair and just to them is often not perceived as such by others. The challenge then, of course, is for foreigners to become familiar enough with Korean culture to mesh the two different value systems and come up with a workable relationship.

Westerners who are new to Korea automatically expect Koreans to react in a *nollijogin* (nuhl-lee-juh-gheen), or logical manner based on their own cultural experiences. However, this often does not happen since Koreans have been culturally conditioned for centuries to react on the basis of personal factors and prevailing circumstances, which may not only be inherently different but changeable. It is therefore necessary to have some knowledge of Korean cultural attitudes and behavior before you can predict their reaction to a given setting, since it may not be "logical" in the Western sense.

The Ethics of Group Consciousness

As noted, traditional Korean ethics had their genesis in Confucianism. One of the outgrowths of this Confucian influence was the emotional and intellectual homogenization of Koreans to the point that *chung* (chuung), or group consciousness, virtually replaced individual awareness.

To make *chung* acceptable to the Koreans, the Confucian dominated Choson Court equated group consciousness with morality, and made it the law of the land. Between 1400 and 1900, the concept of group consciousness became so deeply embedded in the psyche of Koreans that it is still visible today—over 100 years after it was discarded as the "official morality" during the last years of the Choson dynasty.

Chung is visible in present-day Korea—in families and in the workplace. It is, however, no longer the foundation for all Korean actions. The challenge facing foreign managers in Korea is to distinguish between the old morality of *chung* and the new morality—based on the rights and welfare of the individual—in their dealings with employees, suppliers and customers. Generally speaking, Koreans today continue to believe that group consciousness is often superior to the Western cowboy or go-it-alone approach to things, and are adamant in their beliefs.

Chung, or "group consciousness," is also the Korean word for loyalty. But loyalty in the traditional Korean sense was (and often still is) quite different from what the word means to Westerners. Broadly speaking, loyalty in the Western sense is an ethical position based on an unchanging principle whereas loyalty in the traditional Korean sense can be described as "situational ethics." In other words, what is ethical today may not be ethical tomorrow if the situation changes.

This traditional form of ethics is still very much alive in Korean culture because it has proven to be a significant advantage in today's competitive business world. Obviously, this flexibility in ethics can be very disturbing to the Western businessperson who is looking for and expects continuity and predictability in commitments and relationships.

Koreans are especially sensitive to any sign that their foreign partners are not loyal in the Korean sense—which means being willing and able to contend with contingencies that may occur regularly, requiring adjustments in commitments and contracts. It is difficult for foreigners without a deep knowledge of Korean culture to recognize and deal with the various aspects of *chung*. And this is another situation where having an older Korean on staff or as a consultant—to keep both sides on the same cultural channel and accommodating each other—comes in useful.

The "Good Mood" Syndrome

Kibun (kee-boon), meaning "feelings" or "mood," is one of the most important facets of Korean psychology. Koreans are extraordinarily sensitive to slights and setbacks that damage their *kibun* and upset the harmony of their existence, and they will go to what appear to Westerners to be extreme lengths to maintain their own and everyone else's *kibun*.

This conditioned cultural reflex influences virtually every nuance of the private as well as public lives of Koreans and is part of their institutions of etiquette, politeness and respect. The *kibun* factor often plays a decisive role in business because Koreans do not like to give anyone bad news—such news will obviously damage the recipient's *kibun*. This results in a variety of reactions. Unpleasant news or information may be totally withheld, it may be delayed until near the end of the day to avoid spoiling the person's day, or it may be softened, sometimes to the point that it is misleading.

Koreans especially dislike being the bearer of unpleasant news to someone who has a hot temper and reacts emotionally—particularly since they also equate class, breeding and character with keeping one's emotions under control, and responding to any situation calmly. But this latter cultural programming can result in a kind of Catch-22 situation because the demands of Korean etiquette makes them very emotional and subject to reactions that range from subtle to loud outbursts that sometimes turn violent.

In all dealings in Korea, whether personal or business, it is important to keep this facet of the Korean character in mind in order to avoid any unnecessary assaults on anyone's *kibun*.

Dealing with Sensitive Feelings

There are a number of refrains that Westerners doing or trying to do business in Korea (and elsewhere in Confucian Asia) often hear— almost always when some misunderstanding, dispute or difference of opinion occurs, which can be a daily occurrence.

The most common of these refrains is "You must understand the Korean way!" (or the Chinese way or the Japanese way, depending on where you are). In Korea, the outsider cannot begin to grasp the meaning and implications of "the Korean way" without an understanding of the term *kibun* in all of its cultural nuances. Paraphrasing the description of the word in my book, *Korea's Business and Cultural Code Words*: In its full cultural context, *kibun* incorporates most of the values Koreans hold dear. It is the foundation of harmony. It sets the tone, style and quality of all their relationships. Face, dignity, pride, respect and more are bound up in the meaning and role of *kibun*.

For Koreans to develop and maintain harmonious relationships, they must be able to accurately "read" the *kibun* of others, adjust their own expectations and behavior accordingly, and at the same time protect their own feelings.

Richard Saccone says in his book, *The Business of Korean Culture*, that the goal of *kibun* is to help people stay unthreatened, relaxed, comfortable and happy. This makes it imperative that people avoid or ignore many situations that are commonplace in business and everyday life, from minor mistakes and embarrassments to very serious matters.

A person's *kibun* can be damaged by many things that usually involve failure to follow the rules of Korean etiquette. These things include not bowing properly to a superior, failure to use respect language, not using a person's title, unintentionally treating a senior as a subordinate, giving the wrong kind of gift, being the bearer of bad news, criticizing someone in public, questioning someone's veracity or honesty, and so on.

One or more of these failures invariably results in the individual on the receiving end feeling resentment and developing a grudge, and thereafter looking upon the offender as an enemy.

Kibun jo kye (kee-buun joe-kay) refers to the "face" or "manner" that one presents to others to ensure that they will feel good and friendly—something that is crucial in developing and sustaining good relationships in Korea.

Dealing with Powerful Emotions

Western businesspeople who go into Korea without being familiar with the culture are often surprised and sometimes, shocked, at how emotional Koreans can be—often in situations that would not raise an eyebrow in the West.

The reason for this Korean trait is, of course, an outgrowth of Korea's traditional Confucian oriented culture. Until the end of the feudal system in 1910, demonstrations of *kamdong* (kahm-dohng), or emotion, were virtually taboo. Among the few exceptions were demonstrations of affection and love for young children.

Confucianism looked upon love and other expressions of emotion as disruptive to society, and mandated a social system in which emotions were suppressed in the interest of a perfectly harmonious family, community and country.

Of course, this enforced repression of the emotions resulted in the buildup of frustrations and friction that frequently erupted in some kind of violence. But this reaction was rare enough in public for the Korean reputation for being calm and peaceful to remain intact for generations.

Now that the system of official sanctions that kept the lid on the emotions of Koreans for so many generations have been eliminated and the social sanctions have weakened considerably, expressions of *kamdong*—the positive and the negative—are commonplace.

Some of the emotional outbursts of present-day Koreans are collective in nature and involve such things as strikes and other kinds of demonstrations. Other outbursts are personal and often domestic, primarily between husbands and wives.

In business situations, the *kamdong* side of the Korean character generally manifests itself in covert actions against specific individuals within companies. Employees who feel that they have been shamed or wronged in any way will generally not complain openly, but will take some kind of action to punish the offenders.

Identifying disgruntled employees is not always easy, as they can be clever at disguising their feelings. This calls for very sensitive attention to the mix of employees—age, sex, education, birthplace, etc.—plus at least one or more loyal and supportive employees who are tuned into what is going on in an office or workshop, to advise the manager when there is a problem and how to resolve it.

Avoiding the Appearance of Arrogance

Koman (koh-mahn), or arrogance, is one of the many common human traits that was made taboo by Korea's Confucian based government. The edicts applying to *koman* covered those in elite positions, including the king. The higher the position of a person who behaved in an arrogant manner, the greater the sin.

Of course, this does not mean that arrogance was eliminated from Korean society. The power that the social system gave to officials and fathers was such that it bred arrogance in many men. But blatant examples of arrogance were in fact relatively rare, and in extreme cases were fatal to officials who went beyond what people could endure.

The social sanctions against arrogance are not as draconian as they were in feudal Korea, but Koreans remain especially sensitive to such behavior. As it happens, some of the typical behavior of Westerners comes off as arrogant to Korean eyes. These includes bragging, criticizing others, being aggressive in manner and presentations, and making disparaging comments about Korea, Koreans or anything Korean.

The mere fact that a foreign manager insists on something being done exactly as he orders can be taken as arrogance if it suggests that the employee concerned would otherwise not be capable of doing it.

But today, arrogant posturing and arrogant behavior in Korea is not limited to foreigners who have not learned how to function in a cross-cultural setting. Extraordinary economic success by Korea has resulted in some Koreans—in both industry and government—letting their success go to their heads, and their arrogance can be palpable.

Dealing with Korean Nationalism

The etiquette and ethics that Koreans display in their relationships with foreign businesspeople and others invariably have a strong flavoring of *kukkajuui* (kuuk-kah-juu-we), or nationalism.

Korea has a history of over 5,000 years that is marked by numerous invasions by its neighbors and two attempts by the Japanese to totally destroy its indigenous culture. The last invasion of the country by Japan at the beginning of the 20th century was aimed at eliminating both the culture and Korea as a nation. But the Koreans survived all these depredations and became all the more independent minded and strong willed because of them. Their pride in themselves and in Korea is unbounded.

Koreans regard themselves as a unique people and take great pride in using the phrase *uri hanguksaram* (Uh-ree-hahn-guuk-sah-rahm), which means "We Koreans," and is a ringing pronouncement that has racial, cultural, social, geographic, economic and political implications.

Koreans take great pride in the now generally acknowledged fact that it was Korean immigrants who founded Japan's first Imperial Court of record, and that virtually all of the arts and crafts for which Japan is now famous for were introduced into Japan by Koreans. These historical facts help explain the strong nationalism of South Koreans, but not the extreme nationalism of North Korea, which is an aberration that cannot be explained in rational terms. The extraordinary *kukkajuui* of (South) Koreans has played a vital role in the economic success of the country by manifesting itself in the energy and ambitions of the people as well as in government policies that have been formulated to benefit the nation—often at the expense of its trading partners.

These new government policies adopted at the beginning of the 21st century are designed to promote further economic growth and turn the country into a high-tech and cultural hub of East Asia. And while the nationalism exhibited by government agencies and individuals are sometimes a handicap for foreign businesspeople, the Koreans' desire to continue building on their success is so strong that the windows of opportunity for foreign companies in Korea are opened wider than ever.

It is, however, vitally important for foreign businesspeople to understand the sources of the nationalism of the people of Korea, and deal with them diplomatically.

The Western Way vs. the Korean Way

Historically, Europeans and Americans have taken the position that they can do business with anyone, even strangers they have never met and may never meet.

In premodern Korea, however, all relationships—social, business and otherwise—were based on prior relationships resulting from family ties, community, school or work. Any other relationship outside of this circle carried with it a special set of obligations that could range from bothersome and expensive to dangerous. This resulted in Koreans limiting the number of relationships in both their private and public lives.

This facet of traditional Korean culture has weakened considerably since the last decades of the 20th century but it is still a significant factor in the lives of most Koreans, especially the older generations.

Foreigners in Korea generally have a special advantage because they can ignore many of the more subtle obligations involved in meeting and establishing relationships with new people—and get by with it because Koreans do not automatically expect them to behave like Koreans.

But totally ignoring the Korean way in establishing and maintaining business as well as social relationships can be dangerous. It may result in a variety of unpleasant repercussions, as Koreans are culturally conditioned to seek redress (if not outright revenge) for behavior considered unethical or immoral—meaning un-Korean.

What is Fair in Korea?

The ethical and philosophical concept of *kongpyong* (kohng-p'yong), or fairness, did not exist in feudal Korea in the Western sense. The

Confucian social system that prevailed was based on precise hierarchical relationships between inferiors and superiors, and between classes. Confucian ideology did not recognize the principle of equality.

The Koreans' first experience in fairness and equality in human relationships, professional affairs and business did not occur until the introduction of democracy and other Western principles into Korea in the 20th century. Prior to this, inequality was the norm. Social class, political power and wealth now no longer have absolute, government sanctioned priority over human rights and fairness, but *kongpyong* still has a traditional tint in the Korean context of business and politics.

Fairness as a fundamental principle of human rights and behavior has experienced the most acceptance and growth in family and personal relationships. The younger the individuals, the more they have become committed to the principle of fairness in all of their relationships.

In business etiquette and ethics, the level or degree of *kongpyong* in the Western sense varies with the age and size of the company, the age and background of the ranking managers and executives, and depends on whether it is domestic or internationally oriented, and so on.

With the variable exception of individuals who have been educated in the West and/or spent enough years there to absorb the nuances of fairness and equality in their Western context, it is still normal for Koreans to interpret *kongpyong* with a Korean flavor.

This means that foreigners doing business in and with Korea must be sensitive to the possible variations in the understanding and use of the term fairness, keeping in mind that Koreans generally view the concept from their own cultural, social, economic and national perspective. In other words, their fairness may not be a fundamental stand-alone principle that is—or can be—applied universally to any situation.

One attitude of smaller businesspeople in Korea—what they regard as ethically fair—is the notion that they should not be held to the same standards as large companies in their dealings. On a more basic level, Koreans do not believe it is fair or morally right for the US and other larger, richer countries, to demand equal trade rights with Korea.

Since the concept of fairness in Korea is subject to a variety of interpretations, foreign businesspeople—who are generally steeped in the idea of fairness as a universal concept—must be prepared to resolve any issues that arise by either accommodating their Korean counterparts or winning them over to their side.

The Emotional Content of Business in Korea

Western businesspeople should be aware of, and keep in mind, the role that feelings play in Korean behavior. Their emotions are just below the surface and can be turned on with startling suddenness, over something that the outsider might not regard as important.

Behavioral scientists in Korea say this penchant for extreme emotional behavior results from the fact that historically, there was no socially acceptable way for differences of opinion and disputes to be settled by rational discussion and debate.

If a wife wanted to get her husband's attention she had to scream and throw a tantrum. When men wanted to make a point they got drunk and started a fight. If workers wanted to express their displeasure about something, they went out on a strike that often became violent in a controlled and structured way.

This tendency for an emotional eruption is still a part of the character of Koreans. It is generally kept under control by the use of polite and/or laudatory language, and by being especially careful not to do or say anything that others would find offensive.

Another factor in interpersonal relationships in Korea is the use of feelings to persuade, motivate and otherwise manipulate people—rather than using logic and epistemology to win them over.

This factor is often a major stumbling block for the typical Westerner whose approach in business and social situations is to generally use facts and a rational presentation to bring someone around.

Koreans, especially Korean women, are aware of the Western weakness when it comes to dealing with loud and emotional outbursts, and have been known to make use of it to carry the day.

CHAPTER TWO

The Enduring Korean Character

Outwardly, today's Korea is nothing at all like it was in the 1950s, 1960s or even 1970s. Yet, it has changed very little in the underlying principles of society and business. Its liberation from Japanese rule in 1945 and from American dominance in the 1950s was followed by the rapid introduction of a Western facade that has changed the appearance of its cities and to a lesser degree, its countryside.

But this image of scientific industrialism is for the most part, only on the surface. Although thousands of Koreans have been partially de-Koreanized by years of exposure to Westerners—particularly Americans—and other thousands who have been educated abroad are now either bicultural or at least bilingual and able to function in both a Korean and a Western environment, the majority remain identifiably Korean in their basic attitudes and behavior.

The family is still of vital importance. There is still respect for authority, the aged and the learned. All of the "isms" delineated by Dr. Kyong-Dong Kim are alive and well. It is impossible for a Korean or a Westerner to function effectively and efficiently in Korea without following the "Korean way" in many areas of life and work.

Marvin J. Winship, former Director of Operations in Korea for International Executive Service Corps, said: "I have been coming to Korea on business since 1958 and over the years, have had hundreds of conversations about Korean etiquette and ethics in business. The biggest challenge now, it seems to me, is to keep up with the changes, to distinguish between what is still traditional Korean and what has been grafted onto the Korean system from the US or other Western countries. I often need help in understanding the degree of these changes."

Dr. Kim says bluntly that Koreans are still emotional, relatively crude, superstitious and aggressive—but not lazy—and that the Korean society is still organized on an intricate network of personal connections; that it is still an authoritarian hierarchy; that people still resort to ritualistic face-saving facades and emphasize class and rank.

But internal motivation for change, outside pressure for change and the momentum of change are growing rapidly in Korea, and in fact will probably see Korea pull ahead of Japan in its rush to internationalize not only its economy but its society as well. Koreans have never been as ethnocentric, antiforeign, arrogant, militaristic, or determined as the Japanese to spread their way of doing things abroad. This basic difference between Koreans and Japanese will be a major advantage to Korea in its future relations with the world at large.

Humanism and Benevolence in Business

One interesting and important facet of Korean ethics is their traditional commitment to humanistic acts of benevolence—something that probably grew out of their historical experience of living under regimes where life was hard and helping one another was often a matter of survival.

Another aspect of benevolent acts by Korea's ruling class during feudal times was no doubt the "largess of the lord" factor—when they would on certain occasions bestow gifts and other kinds of favors on common people. In any event, the kind of humanism that results in benevolent behavior was characteristic of common people during the country's long feudal history. Korean sociologists say that the core character of the people was subsumed in the word *in* (een), which can be translated as both humanism and benevolence, and they add that the term incorporates the concepts of kindness, meekness and wisdom.

In present-day Korea, this ancient concept of humanism is reflected in attitudes toward the government and toward employers—the idea being what they say and do should be guided by humanistic principles.

The rationale that all work-related situations should conform to the Korean view of humanistic behavior has a direct impact on labor relations in Korea and is something that foreign employers should be aware of.

Defining Korean Management

Korean social science professors and other scholarly types often say there is no such thing as Korean-style *kwalli* (kwah-lee), or management, then go on to describe a system that is typically Korean. What they apparently mean is that there is not one uniform style of management in Korea, but a number of "styles" that differ to varying degrees—mixtures of Korean and Western approaches along with features that reflect the individual philosophies and experiences of their founders or leaders.

The industrial revolution did not get underway in Korea until the Japanese invaded and annexed the country in 1910. The companies set up by the Japanese in Korea as well as those founded by Korean entrepreneurs were patterned after those that had been established in Japan after the 1870s, and were managed like Confucian family fiefs.

It was not until the 1960s and 70s that Korean businesspeople began to import and use Western management practices. Company founders also began sending their sons to business schools in the US and Europe, and by the 1980s, these foreign-educated offspring began showing up in Korean corporations.

But despite the presence of thousands of foreign-educated managers and executives in Korean companies, and the continuing import of Western management technology, Korean *kwalli* continues to be primarily Korean in essence and in flavor.

The structure of Korean companies is still vertical. Management is a combination of top-down and middle management-up, with fewer documents than is common in Japan and the US. Training and discipline are strict. There is virtually no horseplay by employees. Most confrontations and disagreements are settled by edicts from higher up. The emotional content in Korean *kwalli* is high. Corporations are paternalistic.

Promotions and survival on the managerial level is based on survival of the fittest, and competition is fierce. As mentioned earlier, relationships—school ties, blood ties, birthplaces, etc.—play important roles in the politics of Korean companies. Even company events and the travels of senior executives are planned and executed with military thoroughness and precision.

Korean *kwalli* emphasizes sincerity, perfection, absolute loyalty and a willingness to sacrifice for the company, pride in the company and their work, and a serious manner at all times. Many major companies run training programs aimed at breaking down the mindset that employee recruits bring with them, reprogramming them to think and behave as company people with a marine-like spirit.

Managers are charged with the responsibility of training their subordinates in the philosophy of the corporation and in the attitude and behavior that is expected of them, and that of providing them with a variety of incentives to conform and produce. Meetings, speeches and lectures are frequent.

Foreign companies that set up operations in Korea must be aware of and conform to many of the management procedures that are expected—and often required by law. This means having input from a variety of Korean sources, including consultants on the cultural aspect of management in Korea.

Much of the dynamism of the Korean economy during the 1960s, 1970s and 1980s came from the extraordinary spirit, dedication and drive of the numerous founding fathers of the country's business enterprises. They had in common a will to succeed, a missionary zeal and a self-sacrificing dedication that went far beyond the standards of the typically aggressive businessperson. They were also able to instill much of this same drive and dedication in the executives and labor force they had built up to achieve their goals.

These zealous founders did not rely solely on the benefits of the Confucian loyalty and work ethic, however. They also vigorously applied a Korean version of the "carrot and stick" or as it is known in Korean, the *shin sang pil bol*—a form of personnel management, or recognition and incentive, with emphasis on reward and punishment. Winners were pampered and rewarded, while poor performers were subject to harsh disciplinary action.

With the transition from the founders to the second generation of managers, Korean companies began to rely on more traditional approaches, including corporate paternalism that is especially designed to fit the Korean environment. Bonuses, for example, are paid at kim-chi-making time, Chusok (Obon Festival), on the occasion of death in a family or when school fees are due.

Because of the group orientation of Korean society, Korean companies often apply rewards as well as punishments on a group basis too. This has the effect of further forging bonds within the groups and contributes to closer personal ties and cohesion among employees, which in turn result in greater productivity.

"Scold Management"

In a society where criticism and harsh language of any kind has long been one of the strongest taboos, it is something of a surprise to learn that some larger Korean companies use severe scolding and criticism at group meetings as a management technique.

These weekly institutionalized meetings, known as *puseo jang hoe* (puh-say-oh jahng hoh-eh) and conducted by senior managers and/or directors might be termed pep talks, but are in fact like the kind of talks that a loud and brash football coach might give to his under-performing players at half-time. While the frankness and vehemence of the "scold meetings" vary with the personality of the managers conducting them, they are invariably harsh, even to Western ears.

The rationale is that the manager is acting as a father figure who doing his duty to berate his children for failing to perform as diligently and as effectively as they should. And the harsher the criticism is at a particular meeting, the more likely the same manager or director is to later invite the employees out for a drinking party, as a loving father would. This is recognized and acceptable behavior in a strictly Korean setting, but not an approach that foreigner managers should use. Koreans will take such criticism from their own people, but not others.

Another important word in the management vocabulary of Koreans is *tongchal yuk* (tong-chal yahk), or keen insight, a quality top Korean businesspeople look for in managers who are being considered for higher executive positions. The individual with this kind of insight is one who has a conspicuously high level of intuitive intelligence and can be expected to make the right decisions most of the time.

The Mind-Control Factor

Westerners may be put off by any suggestion regarding mind-control. This wariness, however, is not warranted in the Korean context of controlling the mind—it does not refer to an insidious or evil thing.

The Korean concept of gaining control of the mind and disciplining it to achieve goals is subsumed in the word *kyong* (k'yohng), which means something like "humble respect for mind control and the development of reason"—concepts that are both Buddhist and Confucian.

Since AD 1392, Koreans were under very serious social and political pressure to control their emotions and behavior—the latter being in line with the precise rules of etiquette that covered virtually every aspect of their daily lives. The social and political programming for this mind-control became an integral part of Korean culture and was learned since infancy, both by osmosis and by direct teaching. While the cultural programming that present-day Koreans undergo is far less strenuous and extensive than it was before, it is still a major factor in the upbringing, schooling and corporate training that most Koreans undergo.

The influence of *kyong* training remains conspicuously visible in the attitudes and behavior of most Korean employees, managers and executives, who approach their work and goals with extraordinary focus, diligence and perseverance.

The *kyong* concept is one of the sources of the "can do (anything)" attitude that is typical of Koreans—a characteristic that played a leading role in tiny Korea transforming into a major industrial power in one generation. Thus, foreign businesspeople in Korea will soon find that Korean-style *kyong* can be a very positive factor in their relationships with employees, suppliers and others.

Striving for Power

Koreans have always equated *kyoyuk* (k'yoh-yuuk), or education, with power, and with the end of the feudal social system that generally limited learning to the elite upper classes, they have pursued education with an obsessive resolution.

The resolution to learn extends beyond the school stage. It is pursued as relentlessly by businesspeople and professionals throughout their working lives because life in Korea is extraordinarily competitive—and because Koreans view themselves as competing with the rest of Asia and the world at large.

In the 1990s, Korean sociologist Jae Un Kim referred to the Korean obsession with education as a means of elevating their social status as "diploma disease." He said that much of this feeling was a holdover from the Choson dynasty (1392–1910) days during which the ruling class heaped humiliation and degradation on the uneducated lower class.

The Battle for an Education

In Korea, competition for entry into the best high schools and universities is fierce. Virtually all students in the country take the examinations for Seoul National University (SNU) because it is the most prestigious university, and a diploma is practically a guarantee of a desirable career in government or business. Unlike Japan's prestigious Tokyo University, which is public, SNU is a government-run school.

Students who fail in their efforts to enter SNU take the results of the examinations to other prominent universities in declining order of their standing, hoping to at least get into one of them. Most of those who fail to get into any university end up settling for one of the junior colleges.

The most prestigious high school in the country, Kyung Ki, has been in existence for generations. The most elite of the women's colleges is Ehwa (which is sometimes described as the only "real" university for women in Korea).

Just as it has been for the last thousand years, education and schools are of vital importance in establishing the social status of Koreans and determining their careers thereafter. The ties established during high school and college days last through life and become the network by which individuals conduct most of their private and professional affairs. People constantly scan the newspapers and other media for the names of classmates and alumni as possible business or personal contacts.

The competitive spirit that drives Koreans in their education is directly reflected in their etiquette and ethics in business, and therefore impacts on foreigners doing business with and in Korea.

Most Koreans in the business world are far more familiar with Western countries—their history, economics, politics and culture—than Westerners are with Korea, and this gives them a leg up in dealing with the typical American or European…not to mention the feelings of cultural superiority they may derive from this circumstance.

Suffice to say, foreigners determined to undertake the challenge of doing business in Korea should make a serious point of boning up on Korean history as a key part of their initial preparations.

Etiquette as Morality

We have already commented on the fact that for generations, morality in Korea was deeply influenced by Confucian concepts of the structure of an ideal society and how it should be administered through carefully prescribed rules of *yeui pomjol* (yeh-we pohm-johl), or etiquette.

This morality that is based on social etiquette became even more pronounced in 1392, when the newly established Choson dynasty adopted a far more comprehensive form of Confucianism and made it the foundation of both the government and society at large, and thereafter enforced it by law. When the first Westerners visited Korea, they were amazed at the stylish etiquette and dignified behavior of Koreans but at the same time, also astounded that morality in the Western sense did not seem to exist.

Behavior in present-day Korea is based on a combination of Western morality and traditional etiquette, which can be confusing to Westerners who like their morality logical, rational, clear-cut, fair and equally applied to all. However, the etiquette-as-morality approach that prevailed in Korea for centuries is slowly fading away and while foreign businesspeople should abide by the rational courtesies of today's Korea, they should not compromise on moral and ethical issues that are based on sound principles of personal and business behavior.

Koreans, particularly higher-ranking government officials and businesspeople, continue to be very formal in their meetings and receptions.

Their treatment of Westerners also tends to be quite formal. They are especially respectful towards experienced businesspeople and technical professionals, and regard them as teachers in the highest sense.

Like their Japanese neighbors and culturally close kinsmen, the only time Korean businesspeople and government officials dispense with formality is when they are out on the town in informal situations—where drinking is the order of the day.

Dealing with Duty and Obligations

Two foundations of Korea's traditional culture—the concepts and roles of *uimu* (we-muu), or duty, and *uiri* (wee-ree), or obligations, were closely related and often overlapped.

Uimu covered the duty of children to parents, of individuals to their families, of inferiors to superiors, of people to the government and of the living to the dead. These duties were emotional, spiritual and intellectual in nature, and became such an integral part of the mindset of the people that they became a national trait. The duties subsumed under *uimu* took precedence over all personal feelings, including love, as well as all other personal considerations or aspirations.

Uiri, or obligation, differed from *uimu* in that it was extrapolated to include the concepts of absolute integrity, loyalty and the highest standards of Confucian morality, with the goal being to maintain perfect social harmony.

More comprehensive than *uimu*, *uiri* covered the loyalty that parents and children owed to each other, to their kin, friends, elders, teachers, employers and government officials. People were born with *uiri*, and like original sin in the Christian faith, it stayed with one for life. The mandate of *uiri* included all of the etiquette of interpersonal relationships of the living, as well as of one's ancestors.

Uimu and *uiri*—combined with collective responsibility—empowered and directed the Korean society for nearly 500 years, and their legacy continues to influence the behavior of most modern-day Koreans to some degree. While the introduction of democracy and Western-style capitalism into Korea have resulted in a significant reduction in the role and power of *uimu* and *uiri*, both remain readily obvious in the attitudes and behavior of the vast majority of Koreans. Even when doing business with foreigners, most Koreans still aim to create and maintain *uiri*-based relationships, with the emphasis on harmony, loyalty and integrity.

There are, however, exceptions to this rule that generally involve individuals and small companies headed by individuals who do not apply the ethics of *uimu* and *uiri* to their dealings with foreigners, and are charlatans in any language.

Sin Korean-Style

Westerners who do business in Korea should be forewarned that Korean behavior cannot always be judged based on Western concepts of what is right and wrong—especially things that Westerners tend to think of as "sins" in a spiritual sense.

"Spiritual sin" is primarily a Christian concept, and application of this concept to human behavior is limited to the small portion of humanity that has been indoctrinated in Christian morality.

Koreans have, of course, always had a concept of *choe* (choh-eh), which is usually translated as "sin," but *choe*, as influenced by Confucianism, has been more concerned with conforming to the established etiquette than with spiritual matters or keeping the soul pure. It was more of a secular thing than a religious thing.

Anything that upset the hierarchical structure of society or the harmony between the people and the state was regarded as a *choe*. Morality and sin were circumstantial things; not absolute values or principles.

Many Koreans now accept to some degree the Western concept of sin and morality, especially in male-female relations (because in the Western concept men and women are equal), and there are large numbers of Koreans on every level of industry and government who conduct themselves according to Western morality.

But like the Japanese, most Koreans are not religious in the Western sense. Most Koreans continue to follow Buddhist and Confucian customs and rituals—many of them aimed at various gods and spirits—that have been an integral part of their culture for thousands of years.

[This said, a significant percentage of Koreans are in fact, practicing Christians as a result of missionary activity in the country beginning in the late 1800s. Korean women in particular were powerfully drawn to the Christian concept that women have human rights and should not be isolated and forced to serve men as virtual slaves.]

Choe is not related to what happens to the spirit or soul after death. It is what happens in this world that damages individuals, families, friends or society at large.

Generally speaking, all Koreans base their actions not on what is right or wrong from an absolute moral sense, but on what will contribute most to their safety, welfare and success—a criteria that is often much more humane, and more practical than Christian precepts.

The Personal Nature of Business

In Korea, as in many other Asian countries, business is a personal affair. The product, profits and everything else take a backseat to personal relations. If you do not or cannot establish good personal relations with a large network of people, it will be either difficult or impossible to do business in Korea.

Personal relations and contacts, combined with a high sense of honor and trust, are the primary foundations of Korean business ethics. Until recently, written contracts were rare. Most business arrangements were based on verbal agreements. As a result of this system, Koreans spend a significant amount of time expanding and nurturing their personal relations because their business depends on maintaining these relationships.

The foreign businessperson wanting to succeed in Korea must adapt to this system to a substantial degree. It is essential that the foreign businessperson program this kind of activity (and expenditure) into the time frame of his plans and expectations. The more he tries to rush a decision or activity, particularly before the correct personal relationships have been established, the slower the process will be and the greater the likelihood that his efforts will fail.

"Many foreign businesspeople believe that with the right product and price they can easily sell to or buy from any Korean company. This may be the case in Los Angeles or Hamburg but it doesn't always hold true in Korea," said Jon Saddoris, president of METEC, a business consultant firm in Seoul.

"Generally speaking, you are not going to get anywhere in Korea until you establish the necessary 'human relations,'" Saddoris adds. This includes approaching the company in the "correct manner," meaning through an acceptable introduction, and on the appropriate level.

Saddoris says that the first mistake many foreign businesspeople make in their approach to doing business in Korea is to believe that meeting the president of a company and getting his approval and cooperation means smooth sailing from then on. In most cases, the managers—lower, middle and upper—who actually run the company will resent being bypassed and will be less than cooperative, sometimes to the extent that the foreign proposal never gets off the ground floor.

If you have an introduction to the president, it is all right to meet him but you must also meet and establish a satisfactory relationship with the various managers, treating them with the same respect and concern that you extend to the president. This also applies to companies that are still in the hands of founders who appear to make all of the decisions.

In qualifying a Korean company, it is essential that you determine the personal relationships between managers on all levels, especially the relationship between individual managers and directors or the president.

Personal ties such as kinship, the same school, the same birthplace or marriage often take precedence over job seniority, rank or other factors, and may have a significant influence on who actually runs a company and how it is run. A clear understanding of these ties is often necessary to determine who the real decision-maker is in a Korean company that one is dealing with.

Because human relations are so important in doing business with Korean companies, it is vital that you keep up to date on personnel and personal changes within any company concerned. The character and personality of a Korean company is as changeable as the ties and emotions of the people who make up the organization. It is therefore necessary to treat the relationship as a personal one that requires regular stroking and other forms of maintenance.

Although Koreans now readily sign contracts with foreign companies, the contracts are invariably interpreted in the personal rather than legal sense, and generally speaking are no better than the personal relationship that exists between the two parties. If the relationship is not constantly renewed and reinforced, the contract becomes just an ordinary piece of paper.

It is therefore very important for the foreign businessperson going into business in Korea to be personally involved in the process of setting up the operation—which includes obtaining the aid and advice of an experienced Korean to help him make his way through the intricate maze of connections and relationships that are involved.

Once the business operation is established, the need for good, solid personal relations becomes even more important, rather than diminishing. The foreign side cannot sit back and relax as is so often the tendency. This is because the Western habit of relying on contracts and lawyers does not work in the Korean business environment.

Another aspect of the personal approach to business in Korea that often upsets Westerners is the tendency for Koreans to run a company as an extension of a large family, which means they make many decisions that are based on purely personal considerations. Koreans are not likely to significantly change this system any time soon, so the only recourse for Westerners is to learn how to cope with it.

The same personal approach necessary for the smooth functioning of an office or company also applies to a corporation's relations with Korean government officials and bureaucrats. Most companies in Korea assign a particular individual to handle their government relations— invariably a senior member of the company with the most experience in the bureaucratic arena, and "face" with key government officials.

Government bureaucrats in Korea are perhaps even more sensitive to the social and business status of people who approach them, and it is especially important for the foreign company having to deal with them to be aware of this. Sending in a young, low-status person is definitely not the way to go.

More Personal Elements in Korean Business

Americans pride themselves on being able to keep their private and work lives separate—leaving their work at the factory or office, so to speak. Business in this context is kept as free of personal and emotional considerations as possible.

In Korea on the other hand, businesses have traditionally been run as large extended families with little or no separation between work behavior and personal behavior. Throughout the country's long feudal period, the whole of society was based on what Korean sociologists have labeled *sajokuro* (sah-johk-ur-roh), or personalism, and *yonjul* (yohn-juul), or connections.

Business in present-day Korea still has a highly charged personal element and connections are still the life-line of individual businesspeople as well as corporations. People develop and nurture connections all their lives, and use them as key assets. Business management is first and foremost an exercise in harmonizing and directing the emotional makeup of employees. Every business relationship also has a personal-emotional element that plays a leading role in every aspect of its existence.

Foreigners dealing with Koreans must be prepared to make a major emotional investment in establishing and maintaining the kind of emotion-rich relationships that are necessary for success. One might say that the whole of Korean etiquette and ethics is based on conforming to or satisfying the emotional needs first, and the economic needs second.

Another factor that plays a role in the personalized etiquette and ethics of Koreans is little or no recognition of the concept of privacy and confidentiality. It is difficult to keep secrets in a Korean organization. Among other things, it is therefore very important for foreign managers and executives to make sure their personal or private secretaries understand the principle of confidentiality, accept it and will protect it.

Westerners who are ill at ease with business relationships that start out on a personal and emotional level—and generally get more intense as time passes—may not be the best managerial candidates for enterprises in Korea. Still today, it is often said that one cannot understand Koreans and function effectively in Korea without having a good grasp of *in'gan kwan'gye* (een-gahn kwahn-gay), which translates as "interpersonal relationships" and is one of the key phrases used to explain the structure and workings of the Korean society.

While the over-reaching goal of Confucianism was to structure society in such a way that it ensured harmony, the very rules that were designed to control human behavior subverted so many of the natural instincts and aspirations of the people that it simultaneously resulted in deep-seated frustrations, creating friction and potential for disharmony.

In addition to depriving Koreans of the opportunity to think and act as individuals, this system also suppressed virtually all creativity and innovation, and kept Korea in a kind of time warp where nothing changed for many generations.

Although a democratic form of government and a capitalistic economy have released Koreans from the stagnating aspects of Confucianism, the etiquette and ethics that sustained the old system for some 2,000 years became so deeply embedded in the Korean psyche that they remain a significant part of its national character.

In earlier times, individuals who failed to follow the prescribed national etiquette were regarded as "non-persons." These were almost always people who were the lowest on the social order—entertainers, prostitutes, criminals and foreigners. [Foreigners were added to the list because most of the first foreigners to show up in Korea were uneducated and unruly sailors who acted like barbarians when compared to the dignified and formal behavior of Koreans.]

Koreans are still very class and behavior conscious, but there is little if any, covert or overt discrimination against foreigners in general. However, where Korean-foreign relationships are concerned, particularly in business, foreigners are expected to know and abide by most of the ethical guidelines that prevail in Korean society.

Younger Koreans are less conditioned in the Confucian precepts, less well versed in the intricacies of behaving in the traditional Korean way, and typically ignore many of the old rules and customs while in school. But once they enter the working world, whether in private industry or government service, they are required to quickly conform to both the corporate and social culture that prevails in the organization concerned.

One of the facets of contemporary Korean culture—a holdover from the past—is an acute sensitivity to arrogant behavior, or anything that smacks of arrogance. One of the primary principles of Confucianism is the value and importance of a humble mode—from the king or president down to the lowest peasant.

Behaving in a manner that Koreans perceive as arrogant can result in serious repercussions that are generally covert. Unusually skilled and experienced people can demonstrate their abilities on the job quietly and unobtrusively, but if they make a big show and/or brag about them, they become pariahs.

Paying Respect in Korea

Paying respect to parents, elders and others of note in Korea comes under the heading of *jeol* (juhl), and is still prominent enough in the culture to be accurately described as a national trait. This respect takes several different forms and applies to many different occasions—in the use of honorific speech, in bowing, in a deferential manner, in seating arrangements, in who starts to eat first, in gift-giving, etc.

Foreigners visiting or residing in Korea are given some leeway in conforming to the dictates of *jeol*, but it is both polite and wise to learn enough about Korean values and customs to demonstrate respect for its people and their culture. From the viewpoint of business relationships, this is wise because it helps quell the image that many Westerners have of being arrogant in their behavior and insensitive to other cultures.

Besides the business rewards that may accrue from knowing and abiding by *jeol* customs, there is also a personal benefit. It adds a great deal to the ambiance of living and working in Korea when you can fit in and feel at home.

Business success for foreigners in Korea is closely tied to learning and using the respect factor in Korean culture. As with most other key facets of Korean culture, Korean-style *chongyong* (chohn-gyohng), or the concept of paying proper respect, is based on the ideal society promoted by Confucius—which was designed to instill and ensure personal as well as social harmony, and which in turn was based on the suppression of individual interests and desires, and unquestioning obedience to all superiors and authorities.

Until the downfall of feudal Korea (in the mid-1900s) failure to pay the prescribed respect to parents, superiors and government officials was a very serious breach of both etiquette and the law, and in worst-case scenarios, could have disastrous results for individuals and families.

On a personal basis, modern-day Koreans are generally respectful to their parents and other elders by choice, in a formal as well as an informal sense. But in schools and in workplaces, the demands of *chongyong* remain quite strong.

Individuals are normally excruciatingly diligent in paying special respect to their bosses and other seniors in both their behavior and the language they use. Also, Koreans who have not been de-Koreanized by Western influence are acutely sensitive about other people paying them the respect that they believe is due their position, age, sex, education and experience.

Where foreigners are concerned, there is a decided nationalistic flavor to the respect that Koreans expect. Pride in their country and pride in their ancient and recent accomplishments runs deep in Koreans. Any perceived slight is likely to get an emotional response that may be overt or covert, depending on the situation.

Broadly speaking, foreigners, businesspeople and others in Korea must go a bit beyond Western ideas of respect in dealing with employees and government officials in order to avoid ruffling the very sensitive feathers of Koreans.

The Personal Loyalty Factor

As already noted, personal relationships and a minutely prescribed etiquette within social classes defined and controlled virtually all behavior in feudal Korea. This system worked only because an extreme standard of *songshilham* (sohng-sheel-hahm), or loyalty, was imposed on the people, beginning with the family and going on up to the community and clan.

In its Korean context, loyalty was equated with upholding all of the rules and customs that controlled the behavior of individuals and groups, as well as the suppression of all independent thinking and individualistic behavior.

In this environment, loyalty was a personalized thing that depended upon circumstances—not something based on principles—and could therefore change as circumstances changed.

While the feudal family and class system that prevailed in Korea until the middle of the 20th century have undergone dramatic changes, most Koreans today still view and practise loyalty as a personal thing, not as something required by ethics or morality.

In Korean business and politics today, personalized loyalty—to family and classmates in particular—continues to be a major influence that often takes precedence over experience and talent. Expressed another way, Korean-style loyalty frequently takes precedence over logical and rational thinking.

Foreign businesspeople and diplomats dealing with Korea should keep in mind that the emotional content of loyalty generally overrides the logical content. The loyalty of Korean employees often appears to be as much to individual managers and executives, as to companies.

Saving Everybody's Face

Korea was still a deeply Confucian society when World War II ended in 1945. It did not really begin to slough off the centuries of social restraints it had come under until the 1960s and even then, it was generally only the very young who began, little by little, to ignore deeply entrenched social attitudes and behavior.

For more than 500 years, the Koreans had lived in a social system that made a carefully prescribed etiquette the foundation for the national morality—a foundation that was based on sex, age, social class and official position, and conditioned people to be obsessed with making sure that others treated them with an exaggerated level of formal courtesy and respect.

In this system, people became so sensitive to the attitudes and behavior of others that *chae-myun* (chay-me'yun), or face-saving, became one of their highest priorities, taking up a great deal of their time and energy.

This face-saving syndrome incorporated not only the individual, but also the individual's family, and often took precedence over rationality, practicality and the truth. The need for *chae-myun* was so powerful that it influenced every aspect of behavior, especially how language was used. In this environment, speaking directly and clearly became taboo because anything one said that others might take the wrong way, reflected badly on one's highly honed sense of self-respect, propriety and honor.

Histories say that during the long Choson dynasty (1392–1910), the demands of *chae-myun* were so powerful they contributed significantly to cultural, social and economic stagnation because they prevented people from having free, open and critical discussions about things of importance.

During this era, the only safe recourse was to say nothing and do nothing that might upset anyone or lead to changing the way things were done.

Face-saving is still extremely important to Koreans, especially the older generations. Although political and social freedom has unleashed the ambitions and dreams that they had repressed until the 1960s and on, they cannot change things fast enough.

Koreans continuously engage in *chae-myun* in all of their personal and business relationships, and foreigners in Korea must do the same if they wish to succeed. Face-saving remains Korea's "cultural lubricant," without which things cannot and will not run smoothly.

In simple terms, "face" refers to one's social and professional position, reputation and self-image. It is of extreme importance to Koreans that their "face" be protected and maintained. The use of respectful language, the extraordinary degree of politeness, the custom of heaping praise on people and that of massaging their *kibun* (feelings) are parts of the overall process of avoiding any threat to one's self-image—as a man or a woman, as a competent worker, as a professional, or whatever. The downside of this cultural characteristic is that people are excessive in their compliments, avoid being critical when criticism is due, and put much more emphasis on form and appearance than on content or the underlying reality.

The cultural need of Koreans to protect their "face" is often misunderstood by foreigners who are unfamiliar with this kind of etiquette.

Foreign businesspeople should keep in mind that while Koreans as a rule are genuinely friendly and often overly anxious to please, their efforts to maintain their face and that of others in their community can cause serious problems if the foreigner presumes that what he sees and hears is what he is going to get.

Hospitality as Face

Koreans are famous for the hospitality they proffer to *sonnim* (sohn-neem), or guests, and where foreign guests are concerned, this hospitality can be so effusive and aggressive that it can be overwhelming.

One of the primary reasons for such a level of hospitality is that it has long been equated with face or image. The more effusive the hospitality, the more face the host gains. In earlier times, extending profuse hospitality was one of the only ways Koreans had of temporarily dispensing with the enforced frugality of their lifestyle and really enjoy themselves.

Hospitality in present-day Korea, particularly that extended to foreign guests and foreign business associates, has a strong nationalistic element as well as all of its cultural ramifications.

Koreans not only gain personal face by extending an extraordinary level of hospitality to foreign guests, they are also able to demonstrate through such courtesy, unbounded pride in their country, its long culture and its contemporary achievements.

In fact, some degree of Korea's amazing economic achievements can be attributed to the almost compulsive hospitality they extend to their foreign business associates. Most foreigners who regularly visit or take up residence in Korea become deeply attached to the Korean exuberance for life and the almost endless hospitality they receive.

Avoiding Shame

Christianized people around the world are threatened with the fires of Hell if they behave in a way not condoned by their religious leaders. They are taught and conditioned to follow the principles of Christianity based on a deep sense of guilt.

Institutionalized Korean behavior on the other hand, has never been based on divine standards or on a sense of guilt. Instead, it is based on a sense of *changpi* (chahng-pee), or shame, as taught by Confucius.

Confucius was wise enough to understand that guilty feelings can be hidden—that one can be guilty of the most heinous crimes but if not caught and punished, can walk around with his or her head high, neither criticized nor ostracized by friends, family or society at large.

In the Confucian concept, morality was based on one's daily behavior—something that was visible for all to see. Those who did not think and act in an acceptable Confucian way brought immediate shame to themselves, their families and their communities.

In other words, Korean morality was traditionally based on following a prescribed physical etiquette rather than on principles that could be interpreted differently and stretched or ignored without any consequence if one didn't get caught.

The power of a shame culture lies in a natural inclination for people to avoid causing emotional pain to themselves—pain that is caused by being looked down upon by others, by being embarrassed, by being disgraced in the eyes of others and in severe cases, being ostracized from one's family and community.

While there are some similarities between guilt and shame cultures, there are fundamental differences that guilt-ridden people have difficulty accepting. People in shame cultures can get by with all kinds of "immoral" behavior and not suffer the pangs of shame as long as it doesn't become public or as long as it is something that is not considered shameful in their societies.

This means that people in shame cultures can lie, cheat and do other things (that give some Christians fits) without triggering any shameful feelings as long as they follow the prescribed rules of physical etiquette in their relationships with others.

Said another way, feeling shame is primarily a social thing; feeling guilt is more of a spiritual thing. And because of that, shame is a more powerful deterrent to misbehavior than guilt.

Although a significant percentage of Koreans profess to being Christians, and Christian concepts of right and wrong along with its guilt syndrome are well known by Koreans and have had a significant influence on their culture since the end of the 19th century, scratch any Korean and below a shallow guilt layer of Christianity you will find a shame layer of Confucianism. One of the primary rules of doing business successfully in Korea (not to mention dealings with government officials) is never ever shame anyone.

The Unbearable Burden

We mentioned earlier that Korea traditionally had a *mangshin* (mahng-sheen), or shame culture, meaning that behavior was primarily controlled by an extraordinary sense of shame which in fact, was an unbearable burden that they went to extremes to avoid.

This sense of shame—alive and well in present-day Korea although in a significantly reduced form—was a product of Confucianism which taught that the highest morality was abiding by a strict form of etiquette based on hierarchical relationships between people.

The ongoing concern that Koreans have with avoiding shame is one of the cultural factors that often complicates their relationships with Westerners, whose skins tend to be much thicker and often impervious to shame. Among the things that Westerners do—that Koreans are likely to be shamed by—is public criticism, being disrespectful toward them in manner or word, and underestimating their abilities (as perceived by Koreans, of course).

Foreigners doing business in Korea should keep in mind that shame, acutely felt, is far more effective in controlling behavior than the Western concept of guilt, which can be easily contained or ignored altogether, at least in modern times.

The Shame of Failure

Because Koreans were programmed for centuries to shun independent thinking, individualistic behavior and personal responsibility, they became extraordinarily sensitive to personal *shilpae* (sheel-pay), or failure, in any form.

There is a good side and a bad side to the Korean fear of personal failure. On the one hand, it drives them to be wary of personal responsibility and makes them reluctant to think and act independently. But at the same time, it also drives them to work in groups with a diligence and compulsion that often goes well beyond the call of duty from the Western perspective.

Death Before Dishonor

Westerners are familiar with the concept of choosing death over dishonor, but very few people in the West are ever put to the test. The occasions when they do face this challenge are generally extreme situations that more likely than not occur in times of war. In other words, the death before dishonor mindset is not a part of the cultural programming of Westerners.

In feudal Korea on the other hand, ordinary Koreans were taught that upholding their myongye (m'yohng-eh), honor, or not being shamed, was of paramount importance and that without honor they were nothing. And in the Confucian oriented society that prevailed in Korea until the 20th century, upholding one's honor meant scrupulously obeying all of the customs and laws of the society.

In other words, the Confucian concept of honor was not universally applicable, but dependent on the social class, gender, age and position of the individual. These guidelines for what was right and wrong were absolute, and individual interpretations did not exist.

In this context, Koreans became culturally imbued with the belief that they had to uphold their honor at all times, at any cost. This meant they had to conform to the strict etiquette prescribed by custom and the feudal government, dress well and appropriately for their class and station, take all of their obligations seriously, work diligently and hard, be concerned about the reputation of their family, their community, their clan and their country—and to avoid shame at all cost.

Much of the energy and spirit that transformed Korean from a feudal, agricultural society into a world-class industrial power in one generation was derived from their intense feelings of personal and national honor.

To succeed in Korea, foreign businesspeople, and diplomats in particular, must have a significant degree of knowledge about Korean values, expectations and behavior in the context of their ongoing need to maintain their *myongye*.

Peace of Mind

One of the most important ingredients in contemporary Korean culture is subsumed in the world *anshim* (ahn-sheem), which literally means "peaceful heart," but may be translated as "peace of mind."

But the "peace of mind" inferred by *anshim* does not refer to the universal concept of harmony in thought and behavior in the Western sense. It refers to obeying the precise rules and customs of Korean behavior so that there is no friction between people, no disputes, no fights and no hurt feelings.

Anshim remains the ideal of contemporary Korean culture and much of the social and business etiquette as well as the ethics of Korean behavior are designed to create and sustain an environment of "peace of mind" in personal relations, business and other public activities. Even the Korean language itself is a primary vehicle for creating and sustaining *anshim*, in both the vocabulary that is used and the manner of its use.

A great deal of the Korean behavior that outsiders consider irrational, ignorant or disruptive in some way is a manifestation of the deep-seated need of Koreans to maintain the culturally mandated *anshim*.

Some examples of this behavior: an employee who keeps quiet about a mistake; an employee who does not complain about an obvious injustice and businesspeople (as well as politicians) who misrepresent the facts to avoid upsetting *anshim*.

Anshim often demands that Koreans express themselves indirectly—keeping quiet when Westerners would speak up, and then expecting others to understand their true meanings and feelings from their common cultural background.

Koreans, like most Westerners, are also culturally blind in that they generally expect foreigners to understand and accept their culturally induced behavior because that is the only way they can think and behave.

Much of the communication in Korea is nonverbal and subliminal—and equates very well with what I call "cultural telepathy." There are certain things that people do and certain rules they obey that do not require conversation or explanation. They are simply understood and accepted without question.

Foreigners in Korea can overcome some of the obstacles caused by the dictates of *anshim* by letting their Korean friends, contacts or co-workers know that they are familiar with the requirements of *anshim* in Korean life, and will do their best to abide by them.

Situational Truth

The first Westerners arrived in Korea in the 1600s as a result of their ships floundering on the Korean coast in raging storms. When the survivors were finally allowed to leave the country—or managed to escape—they had one complaint in common: that Koreans were incapable of telling the truth.

What these early castaways had encountered was a culture in which *chongmal* (chohng-mahl), or truth, was situational or circumstantial, and was based on existing realities of Korean life—not abstract principles. Truth was what the government and people in power said it was. The people of Korea at that time were simply not allowed to speak the truth in their personal relationships or any of their affairs—much less about things directly controlled by the government.

In my book, *Korea's Business and Cultural Code Words*, I described this situation in the following terms: "The 'truth' in all matters was an artificially constructed political and social artifice that had been designed to preserve the harmony of a hierarchically arranged authoritarian society that denied personal individuality and human rights. All personal feelings and concerns were secondary to the interests of the state, which based its policies on a corrupted form of Confucianism that the government used to justify itself."

In such an authoritarian environment, a "truthful" response was whatever that would sustain and enhance the harmonious actions and reactions of the people within its culture—one in which the attitudes and actions of the people were carefully controlled, right down to how to hold chopsticks.

When these earlier Western visitors encountered this form of Korean reality, they took it to mean that Koreans had no principles and no honor, and that they knowingly lied for malicious purposes rather than as a part of their normal behavior.

Present-day Koreans are perfectly aware of the differences been real truth and contrived truth. When they are in "culture free" situations, as when they are dealing with foreigners, their inclination is to tell the real truth. But when they are in purely Korean settings, they are under tremendous pressure to tailor the truth to maintain Korean-style harmony—to keep everything calm and smooth on the surface.

This ancient way of maintaining harmony is being eroded by the dictates of a society that is less and less controlled by Confucian ethics, and more influenced by the hard facts and realities of democracy and capitalism. Still, the foreign businessperson or diplomat in Korea must have his or her "truth antenna" up at all times in order to avoid being misled, intentionally or otherwise, by the legacy of circumstantial truth that still lingers in the culture.

Justice Korean-Style

It often seems that the most popular word in the vocabulary of American businesspeople dealing with Korea and other countries is "fair." This is especially interesting because until recent times, there was no word in the Korean (or Japanese!) language for the word "fair."

In feudal Korea (which did not officially end until late 1945 and was unofficially still present until the 1960s and beyond), the concepts of equality and fairness did not play any role.

Americans in particular have traditionally tried to enforce fairness with a justice system that has only been partially successful, but is better than nothing. In Korea, the traditional justice system had an altogether different foundation and purpose. It was designed to sustain the government and ruling powers, and to maintain a strict kind of harmony based on Confucian concepts.

In other words, *chongui* (chohng-we), or justice, was designed by and for the government, to keep the people under absolute control. Both responsibility and punishment were collective and often severe—something that virtually prevents innovation and progress.

Justice and fairness in the contemporary Western sense did not exist in Korea until well after the end of the Korean War in 1952, when Korean students began taking to the streets in massive and often violent demonstrations demanding that the laws be changed. It took many years, but it was high school and college students in Korea who forced government leaders to break with traditions that went back thousands of years.

Justice and fairness in Korea still have a nationalistic tint. In some business cases, they are aggressively tilted in favor of Korea and Koreans, so it behooves foreigners doing business with Koreans to be very aware that the words justice and fairness do not necessarily mean the same thing in Korean terms.

Generally, justice in Korea is based on what its judges and government agencies believe is best for Korea as a country and for Koreans as a people—from the viewpoint that in the past, Koreans have suffered massive death and destruction at the hands of foreign powers and ideologies.

Another factor in regards to justice and fairness in Korea: there are regional differences that impact on business, sometimes to the detriment of foreign companies. It is thus important for foreigners to get local input from friendly staff or others who can help them adjust to local conditions.

The Communications Problem

Communication is, of course, a necessary foundation for understanding and cooperation, and while more and more Koreans are being educated abroad and becoming bilingual, and the number who learn English in local schools is also increasing rapidly, the foreign businessperson who does not learn some Korean is greatly limited in both his professional and social contacts in Korea. Those who cannot communicate at all in Korean are severely handicapped in their ability to relate to and participate in life outside the narrow confines of the foreign community and world of international business.

Korean is generally described as difficult for English speakers to learn because it is unlike any Western language. Becoming really fluent in Korean is a formidable task, but learning enough of the language to communicate on a basic level is easy. Anyone of average ability can accomplish this limited goal in two or three months of daily sustained study. Korean is mostly made up of "pure Korean" and Chinese words, along with a sizable number of terms borrowed from Japanese and English. The Korean language is called *hangugo* (hahn-guu-go) in Korean. The alphabet, created by a team of scholars in the 1400s at the behest of King Sejong, is called *hangul* (hahn-guul). There are 14 consonants and ten vowels in the language. Various combinations of these make up approximately 54 sounds or syllables. [See the back of this book for a list of these syllables and a pronunciation chart.]

Over the centuries, very few Westerners learned the Korean language, resulting in Koreans believing that the language was simply too difficult for foreigners to learn. As recently as the 1970s, Korean-speaking Westerners were so rare that most Koreans were amazed to encounter one who was able to speak the language—and they would often fail to understand the Korean-speaking foreigner because they simply couldn't conceive of that being possible.

Anecdotes of Westerners speaking relatively fluent Korean but getting only a blank stare in return were commonplace. This situation has changed considerably since the 1970s, however. A significant percentage of the foreign businesspeople stationed in Korea are students of the language and some of them speak it very well. Koreans in rural areas may still be surprised to hear Korean spoken by a foreigner, but this is no longer the case in the cities.

Because of the development of a superior-inferior social structure and a highly refined system of etiquette between and among classes of people, several different levels of language were also developed to distinguish between individuals and classes. The three most important basic levels of the language are: an extraordinarily polite form used when addressing superiors, an intimate or familiar form for addressing close friends or equals, and a rough form used when speaking to people on a lower social level.

Becoming fully fluent in Korean therefore means that one has to master these various levels, which is almost like learning three related but different languages. Fortunately, foreigners who are less than fluent are generally excused from this very strict social requirement and can get by with the use of familiar Korean in most situations. There are occasions, however, when the use of familiar speech is not appropriate and it is better either to speak in English or to remain silent.

As is often the case in Asian languages, there are a number of peculiarities in Korean and its usage that must be quickly mastered by the foreigner who attempts to use the language on any level. It is very uncommon to use the single word "no" as a response, since it is regarded as too abrupt and impolite. In Korean, the appropriate response to a negative question is a positive—in other words, if you say "Don't you know his phone number?", the answer may be "Yes." (Meaning "Yes, you are right. I don't know his phone number.")

This can cause both confusion and frustration, and can be avoided by phrasing all questions in the positive form. "No" is one of the most commonly used words in the English language, but it is virtually untranslatable in Korean and gives a very negative image when used—because Koreans tend to associate its use with being uncertain and unable to make up one's mind.

Until the 1980s and 90s, American expatriates were notorious for not knowing and not making any attempt to learn local languages. That ignoble part of the American mindset has finally yielded to logic—virtually all American businesspeople stationed in Korea now avid students of the Korean language.

The Korean standard for communicating with others is expressed in the phrase *uishin jonshin* (we-sheen joan-sheen), which literally means "from my heart to your heart" or "heart to heart." In its Korean context, it is the type and level of communication that takes place nonverbally, and is a kind of cultural telepathy.

Because they are products of an intensely personal and homogenized culture, Koreans often know what the other person is thinking without the use of words. It is the type of communicating they are naturally familiar with, and they often run into difficulty in dealing with foreigners because they take for granted that the foreigner is on the same wavelength and is "receiving" their messages.

The Great Ethical Divide

The one ethical area that probably causes Western businesspeople more frustration than anything else in the Korean social system is the dichotomy between fairness and loyalty. To Westerners, particularly Americans, the bedrock of their ethical philosophy is fairness. This word is probably used more often than any other in our business discussions and negotiations.

In Korea, however, personal loyalty often takes precedence over fairness. When this difference in ethical codes is applied to business relationships, the results are very different, to say the least. It is therefore vital that the foreign businessperson keep this distinctive Korean cultural value in mind at all times so that he may anticipate the effect it will have on everything he does in Korea, from dealing with government officials to haggling with a landlord over the cost of an apartment.

This is another area in which Western businesspeople with limited cross-cultural experience typically make one error after another—by either ignoring the fairness-loyalty factor altogether or playing it down—because their inclination is to believe that everyone automatically understands and appreciates the concept of fairness, and will just as automatically accept it as the foundation for any business relationship.

The Kindness Trap

Koreans are legendary for their kindness and hospitality. It is one of their strongest cultural traditions—and is now used unabashedly in their diplomacy and business dealings with the rest of the world. Foreign visitors are entertained and pampered, often to the point that they are no longer able to make objective decisions. This gives Koreans a tremendous advantage, especially where Americans are concerned, since we feel such an overwhelming obligation to reciprocate by being less critical and more cooperative in helping them achieve what they want.

Since it is both financially and emotionally difficult for the foreign visitor to match the generosity of Korean hosts, it frequently becomes necessary to limit the amount of hospitality one accepts, and to take extra steps to get even with some kind of special gift.

Class Consciousness and School Ties

Americans and other Westerners are racial and color conscious, but Americans are generally not class conscious—something that can have a negative impact on their hiring and managing employees in Korea.

Unless cautioned and informed by someone with cultural experience in Korea, foreign managers are likely to encounter problems as a result of the ongoing existence and role of social class in any group of Korean employees they employ.

In the past, American managers who had some knowledge of Korean culture have attempted to preempt future problems by lecturing their Korean employees on democracy, and informing them that class would play no role in the management of the company.

While Korean employees surely understood and appreciated the principles of such lectures, the lectures invariably had little, if any, effect on their attitudes and behavior—both being deeply embedded in their psyche and not subject to being switched off at will.

While the cultural character of younger, educated Koreans has changed and continues to change, in virtually any group there will be class differences that continue to influence the behavior of every individual in the group.

Newcomers setting up operations in Korea should get local input in both hiring and managing a Korean staff, preferably from a professional employment agency instead of through personal contacts.

Another key factor in successfully managing employees in Korea already mentioned several times, is utilizing the bonds of *tongchang hoe* (tohng-chahng hoh-eh), or alumni groups. School ties, especially that among individuals who attended the same schools from primary grades through to university, are especially strong, often approaching the importance of blood-ties.

Within large companies that hire from the same schools, these groups form generational layers based on longevity—a factor that perpetuates the junior-senior relationship throughout their working lives, and generally contributes to cooperation, loyalty and diligence in the attitudes and performance.

These same generational layers of alumni groups also play a vital role among companies, since they facilitate communication and cooperation among the companies.

Foreign companies going into Korea should be aware of this factor, and take advantage of it by hiring graduates from schools with graduates who are well-placed in business and the government.

Corporate managers and executives who have junior alumni brothers in high government offices have a special advantage, since the etiquette and ethics that control junior-senior relationships in Korea remain a powerful force in society.

Juniors and Seniors

Despite the Western façade presented by contemporary Korean society and its business infrastructure, once you get behind, or beneath, the façade many of Korea's traditional cultural customs and habits are still very much in evidence.

One of the most important cultural factors in feudal Korea's hierarchically structured society was the *sonbae* (sohn-bay) and *hubae* (huuh-bay), or senior-junior system of ranking people. In this system, there were no equals. Everyone except the king was higher or lower than somebody else, and this gradation determined the individual's life to an incredible degree.

All of the traditional factors that determined one's status in terms of *sonbae* and *hubae* are still in use in contemporary Korean society, although in weakened form in certain areas. These factors include sex, age, family background and schools attended.

Again, Korean companies and other organizations function very much like army or marine corps squads—companies, regiments and divisions, with corresponding ranks based primarily on the above factors, plus longevity. Upper level managers and executives are invariably made up of individuals who come from elite family backgrounds and the ranking high schools and universities.

Differences in rank within organizations of all kinds are taken seriously and the behavior of people on all levels is regimented just as it is in military life. The social credentials as well as attitude and behavior play a role in promotions to upper levels of management.

Foreign companies hiring staff in Korea should be well informed about the social and educational background of applicants because their background will influence the way others view and treat the company. Foreign managers should also be wary of hiring and mixing staff whose backgrounds are dissimilar in order to avoid possible friction.

One source of potential problems is to put someone of a lower social rank over an employee whose social pedigree—class and education—is higher. This may be done, however, if the higher ranked employee is significantly older and obviously more experienced than the other individual.

Korean companies make every effort to take advantage of the obligatory ties that exist among senior and junior graduates of the same high schools and universities, since these ties mean they are much more likely to be loyal and work together smoothly.

Foreign companies setting up in Korea are advised to get professional assistance in formulating their work rules and in hiring personnel to avoid cultural missteps. They should also be wary of depending on a single Korean contact they may have to line up employees, since he or she is likely to pick family members, relatives and friends.

The Power of Social Debts

Another of Korea's cultural legacies from its Confucian past is expressed in the term *unhye* (uhn-heh), which means "benefits," and is extrapolated to cover the "social debts" that people incur and are under a heavy moral obligation to repay.

Unhye covers the debt that people owe to their parents, teachers, schoolmates, employers—anyone, in fact, from whom they have received a benefit that contributes to their livelihood and life goals.

Parents and teachers in particular have a strong moral right to expect that those whom they have benefited will repay them throughout their lives. University professors traditionally use their influence with former students in high positions in government and industry to hire or find jobs for newly graduated students, thus continuing the circle of *unhye*. Foreign businesspeople and others can build up the same kind of "social capital" by doing favors for individual Koreans and their families. Acting as the host for a Korean student studying abroad ensures that the family will do everything possible to repay the benefit.

The Stubborn Syndrome

A national attribute of Koreans that all foreigners encounter at one time or another—and often on a daily, ongoing basis—is a natural propensity for *ogi* (oh-ghee), or stubbornness.

It seems obvious that the stubbornness that characterizes Koreans is a legacy of all the hardships they had to endure over the millennia, from the weather and other natural disasters to occupation by foreign invaders and the pain and suffering imposed on them by their own governments.

The literal meaning of *ogi* is "unyielding spirit," and that describes Koreans to a T. Among the manifestations of this stubbornness is an unwillingness to admit to making a mistake, or to admit that they are not capable of doing something.

These two attributes are, of course, exactly the opposite of the etiquette and ethics of Americans and Western Europeans. Our way is to admit mistakes, do everything possible to minimize any damage, and get on with it.

Koreans typically take great pride in their stubbornness, seeing it as the quality that has allowed them to survive and to succeed where so many others have failed. Still, Korean businesspeople are very much aware that this cultural factor is often upsetting to foreigners, and they continuously counsel patience. They also typically add that to succeed in Korea, you need an iron butt (because of so many long meetings) and an iron stomach (to take all of the alcohol that is typically consumed in the process of establishing and keeping business relationships in Korea).

There is no simple or short way of getting by the *ogi* of Koreans. It is a deeply embedded state of mind that yields only gradually to patience and persistence—if ever. The decades-long *ogi* of the North Korean government is as good or as bad as it can get, depending on which side of the demarcation line you are on.

Doing Things by the Book

Westerners, Americans in particular, are familiar with the saying, "doing things by the book"—which seems to be most commonly used in the military and in law enforcement, where personal thinking and initiative is frowned on.

Well, Westerners who do things by the book are babes-in-the-woods when compared to the Koreans. For some 2,000 or more years in Korea, there has been an exact and precise *chongshik* (chohng-sheek), process or procedure for doing things, for virtually every action in life.

To paraphrase my description of this culturally laden term in *Korea's Business and Cultural Code Words*: "For centuries, the Koreans were physically, emotionally and intellectually programmed in all of the *chongshik* making up the Korean lifestyle—from worshiping, bowing, sitting, eating, working, performing household chores to the way they used their language."

This conditioning in attitudes and behavior was so pervasive that it gradually became the foundation of the Korean lifestyle, so integrated into Korean culture that the two could not be separated. It was something that was automatically taught to each child directly and indirectly from infancy, and thus became an integral part of his or her character and personality.

Most Koreans today still do things "by the book" to a much greater degree than Americans and other Westerners. It is still very much a part of formal ceremonies, business and diplomatic protocol, cultural rites, festivals, etc.

This ongoing cultural factor may not be inherently bad, but it often formalizes meetings and other endeavors to the point that it becomes a serious drag on efficiency, spontaneity and innovation. Even the most mundane things often must be "done by the book," almost always resulting in complications and delays.

Again because of the dictates of democracy, capitalism and an economy that is rapidly becoming global, major corporations and the Korean Government are making a serious effort to reduce the formality and complexities of many procedures.

But Koreans as a whole are not likely to disavow all of their traditional *chongshik* because they are too integrated into the Korean lifestyle and culture. It still defines the character and behavior of most Koreans.

Dealing with Facts

Western businesspeople love facts; Koreans typically put human feelings first. The gap separating the two sides can therefore be enormous. Even when the gap is narrow, it can blunt the building of a new relationship and gradually undermine one that has been going on for years.

Another gap that often separates Westerners and Koreans is the Western concept of fairness. What is fair to a Westerner may not be fair to a Korean. Fairness in the Korean mindset tends to be based on personal factors; not on the hard, dry facts, mutual equality and mutual benefits that motivate Westerners.

In Korea, fairness was traditionally based on class, sex, age and position, with all of the inferior-superior elements that made up their hierarchical society. Much of this mindset has gone by the wayside, but there are still fundamental differences in the way Koreans and Westerners measure fairness.

Foreign businesspeople in Korea can generally work around this difference by first emphasizing the personal, human elements of their relationship and the personal facets of projects or programs, and then bringing in the facts of the situation.

Handled with diplomacy and a true appreciation of the feelings of Koreans, it is almost always possible to get down to the hard facts of a relationship that includes the full understanding and cooperation of the Korean side. It is more in the presentation than absolute differences in methods and goals.

When Maybe Means No

For centuries, Koreans were meticulously programmed to avoid confrontations, ultimatums and clear-cut commitments as a means of ensuring harmony in society. To achieve this goal, the people were conditioned to speak in vague terms that could be interpreted in a number of ways, or not to speak at all.

In the country's hierarchically structured society and with absolute rules controlling inferior-superior relationships, speaking in clear, unambiguous terms, telling the truth or making a negative comment could have seriously negative repercussions and in worst-case scenarios, be life-threatening.

In this environment, Koreans learned to avoid saying "no," and to divine the meaning and intent of others through cultural intuition, or "cultural telepathy." Saying *anio* (ahn-n'yoh), or "no," outright was regarded as impolite, if not insulting.

When the first Westerners to visit Korea encountered this kind of behavior, they immediately assumed that Koreans were dishonest, devious and could not be trusted.

The social imperative for ambiguous speech has eroded significantly in contemporary Korea, especially among those who are involved in international business. But it continues to be an important cultural factor in business and politics, and must be taken into account.

One of the obvious ways to bring negotiations to a close and get clear-cut commitments, is to ask that they be put in official documents that are signed by the responsible people. If the documents are not forthcoming, the real situation is clear.

Personal Responsibility

It was not until the 1960s and 70s that Koreans began to win and receive the right to behave as individuals for the first time in the long history of their country.

Prior to these fundamental changes in Korean society, the people were simply not allowed to think or act like individuals. They were bonded to their families, communities, the authorities and traditional customs, and had to act in unison with them.

Under this system, individual Koreans could not develop a sense of personal *chaegim* (chay-geem), or responsibility. Responsibility was collective—based first on the family, then on the community, then the clan. The father and the family as a whole were responsible for the attitudes and conduct of every member of the family—not only in enforcing the laws and customs of the day, but also in accepting collective punishment when any member behaved in a disruptive manner.

Present-day Koreans are still conditioned to believe in collective responsibility—a factor that impacts directly and fundamentally on their social and business behavior, and often puts them at odds with Western thinking and expectations. In broad terms, Westerners expect individuals to take personal responsibility for their attitudes and actions while Koreans continue to take a more collective approach to all *chaegim*, especially in work-related situations.

Korean executives and managers generally give an impression of authoritative figures who can and do give orders on their own because they are invariably surrounded by cadres of secretaries and aides who would respond to their orders like marine recruits. But in reality, it is generally only strong-minded company founders who can give orders like a military commander.

While there is a gradual shift in some companies to decision-making by individuals, most executives and managers can act only after they have achieved a consensus within their departments or divisions.

More and more Koreans are also assuming personal responsibility for their actions in family as well as business affairs, but it will surely be a number of generations before the influence of collective *chaegim* has diminished to the point that it has in the West.

Dealing with "Big Brother"

In Korea, the national interest often takes precedence over private business, and the government plays a key role in most industries by significantly influencing or outright controlling who can do what and how it is done. The government exercises its influence and control through a variety of laws, long precedents, and the willing cooperation and support of much of the Korean business community.

The objective of the Korean government is to do every thing possible to encourage the rapid and rational growth of the economy and development of the national infrastructure so the entire nation benefits, rather than allow a free-for-all atmosphere which results in extraordinary growth in some areas but disruptions or deteriorations in others.

Within the context of this overall government policy, individual businesspeople and enterprises are allowed the freedom to grow as fast as they can and make as much profit as possible. To keep industrial and social development going forward in the direction it desires, the government makes ready use of all of its powers.

Some of the methods used by the government—and by Korean companies in their dealings with foreign partners—to get its way are to impose import or export restrictions, to deny or delay licensing applications, to cause customs clearance difficulties, to refuse to renew visas, to stop payments, to break contracts and so on.

Despite the real and apparent handicaps this policy represents to foreign companies wanting to do business in Korea, the overall climate for foreign investment and business activity in Korea is favorable, and offers special opportunities to those who are able and willing to approach the market with an open mind, goodwill, a great deal of flexibility, determination and patience.

At the same time, there are many Korean businesspeople, government officials and others who are strongly opposed to welcoming any more foreign businesspeople in the country because of the potential danger to its security and continuing economic success—in direct contradiction to the public policies of the government. These sentiments are often responsible for the "invisible barriers" that foreign businesspeople frequently encounter in Korea.

Because these conflicting positions and practices further complicate the relationship between businesspeople and government, it is vital that the foreign businessperson who hopes to succeed in Korea understand the psychology of Korean behavior as well as master some of the techniques for dealing with individuals on many levels and in a variety of different ministries or agencies.

The first and probably most important lesson the foreign businessperson must learn is that individual government officials cannot be approached on a strictly rational, practical or policy basis. Everything is handled on a case-by-case and very personal basis. Furthermore, officials on different levels in the same agencies and ministries will interpret the same laws and factors differently, often resulting in substantial delays before an application or proposal can be steered through the government red tape.

Probably the second most important lesson is that neither the ethical nor the legal system in Korea provides the kind or depth of security and protection that the typical Western businessperson is used to and expects. This includes the view and treatment of contracts, patents, copyrights and other legal matters.

The third most important lesson may well be that even after everything has been approved and seems to be in order, the whole thing can come apart and have to be renegotiated because in the view of some government official or company executive, circumstances have changed and the original agreement is no longer valid.

This means, of course, that the successful businessperson in Korea must remain in regular communication with everyone even remotely connected or involved in his business, in order to remain current on their thinking and plans to be able to anticipate their actions.

Again, this comes down to establishing and nurturing personal relations with company managers and government officials on all the appropriate levels, in all the concerned ministries or agencies. This entails a great deal of the individual's personal time as well as expenditures for drinks, meals and other expenses. The developing and nurturing of personal relations of this type cannot be done casually or taken for granted. It is a serious business.

Another aspect of the personal side of business in Korea is that the foreign businessperson, no matter what his experience or credentials in his home country, must "re-prove" himself in Korea in terms that are acceptable to Koreans. He must earn the respect and loyalty of Korean associates and employees through his professional skills and knowledge, through his approach to developing and maintaining the expected personal relations, by not breaking any of the taboos of Korean society, by demonstrating sincerity and appreciation for Korean sensitivities, etc.

It is especially important for the foreign employer in Korea to treat his Korean staff with enlightened, personal concern that keeps them loyal and motivated. This includes following expected procedures in management and otherwise in dealing with employees.

The Guiding Hand of Government

In the words of a foreign businessperson with long experience in Korea, "the government is everywhere," meaning there is virtually no area of business that is free of governmental influence or outright guidance.

The Korean term for the influence the government exercises over business matters is *haengjung chido* (hang-jung chee-doh), which means "administrative guidance." This influence is exercised through the control of licenses, import and export quotas, taxes, government financing and so on. In addition, there are also numerous *naekyu* (nay-k'yuu) or unwritten laws, that agencies and ministries use to influence and/or control the economy.

One of the unwritten laws that many businesses, Korean and foreign, encounter, goes by the picturesque name of *gara muingeida* (gah-rah muun-gay-dah), which translates as "crushing with one's rear end," in other words, killing applications or proposals by sitting on them until the petitioner gives up.

Another descriptive term for government inaction is *jajungga bakwi dolligi* (jah-juung-gah bahk-wee dohol-lee-ghee), or "pedaling on a stationary bike."

The *naekyu* may or may not be applied, and may also be applied in a different manner or to different degrees by different individuals. This is one of the reasons why it is so important for foreign businesspeople to have the input and guidance of someone who has been on the Korean business scene for a long time and knows how to get around and through the maze of *naekyu*.

Another factor in the lives and fortunes of business in Korea is the presence of hundreds of *hyopoe* (h'yahp-poh-eh), or associations, many of which are sponsored by the government and therefore quasi-government agents.

There is an association for virtually every industry and profession in Korea, all of which are required to operate within guidelines established by the government. But not all of them are burdensome to business. Some maintain extensive data banks of information on specific industries and provide free staff help to businesspeople seeking such information, as well as assist them in setting up appointments.

The government and the state-sponsored associations also follow the age-old practice of bringing political, economic and social leverage against companies to prevail upon them to make *kibu* (kee-buu), or donations, to various causes.

According to the local press, many of these donations end up in the pockets of politicians and political parties.

While the machinations of the Korean government and its agents are often criticized by local and foreign businesspeople, the overall results of this "Big Brother" approach to the economy has been a major factor in Korea's rise to economic prominence.

The Role of Friends in Business

One of the primary keys to doing business successfully in Korea—and enjoying the process—is having lots of *chingu* (cheen-guu), or friends.

Having a wide circle of friends and friendships is something new to Korea. During the long Choson dynasty (1392–1910), and for that matter, during the Japanese occupation of Korea from 1910 to 1945, friends and friendships outside of one's family and kin were rare.

During the Choson period, men and women lived virtually separate lives. Relationships of women were especially limited to members of their own families and close kin. In urban areas, women were confined to their homes during the day and could only visit female relatives for a few hours at night, when men were required to stay indoors. Social customs also restricted the relationships of men to a narrow circle.

This factor was one of a number of things that limited economic, political and social progress in Korea until modern times. It was not until the feudal class system was abolished and the introduction of Western type companies into Korea at the end of the 19th century that the limitations on friendships outside of family and kin circles began to break down—and this applied mostly to males.

Despite all of the changes that have occurred in Korea, especially since the end of World War II and the occupation of Korea by Japan, establishing new friendships in Korea is not the casual thing that it is in the West. Except among the young, it is still regarded as a matter that requires serious thought because of obligations that might result.

But because Koreans do not feel comfortable or safe in doing business with strangers, they have literally been forced to go out and establish friendly relationships with large numbers of people in industry and in the government—something they do deliberately and with caution, after planning the move.

Koreans do not have any qualms about quickly establishing relationships with foreigners because there is little or no cultural baggage attached to such friendships. They are, however, discriminating in who they become friends with. Foreigners whose character, personality and attitudes do not measure up to their standards don't make the cut.

The Importance of Sincerity

Cultural gaps between Koreans and foreigners, especially Westerners, are often wide enough for inexperienced and insensitive people to fall into them. One of the problems that both sides have to work to overcome is the perception that the other side is not to be trusted.

In judging others, again especially Westerners, Koreans generally put *chinshim* (cheen-sheem), or sincerity, high on the list of required attributes. Those who do not measure up to the standards expected by Koreans will not have an easy time of it.

The catch comes with what Koreans mean by *chinshim*—which, as it turns out not surprisingly, is often quite different from what Westerners mean by sincerity.

To Westerners, being sincere means being open, honest and straightforward. To Koreans, being *chinshim* (which literally means "true heart") is being true to all of their cultural expectations; that is, a person who is *chinshim* will be unselfish, unscrupulously honest, loyal to superiors, hardworking and willing to make whatever sacrifices are necessary to succeed in any work or enterprise.

Expressed another way, being sincere in the Korean context means not doing anything that would harm or shame others; not doing anything that would damage an enterprise or a relationship; not rocking the Korean boat—a concept that is quite different, and much more comprehensive, than the Western perspective.

This means that the foreign businessperson who wants to be accepted as *chinshim* must be able and willing to do things the Korean way—or be well enough versed in the ins and outs of Korean culture to explain his or her perspective in terms that are acceptable to Koreans and that will benefit rather than damage the enterprise.

Koreans automatically measure the *chinshim* of everyone they meet, and their "sincerity" radar is tuned up to the maximum when they meet foreigners for the first time.

Foreigners who want improve their chances of making a good impression on new Korean contacts can do so by commenting that they are well aware of the importance of *chinshim* in establishing and maintaining a positive relationship, and are committed to it.

The Self-Reliant Syndrome

One of the most interesting and significant terms in the vocabulary of Korean businesspeople and politicians is *juche* (juu-cheh), which may be translated as self-reliant or self-sufficient.

The concept of *juche* is especially interesting because until well into the 20th century, Koreans were not permitted to be self-sufficient. The majority had to produce their own food and clothing but beyond that, what they could do was strictly limited by law and by tradition. Further, the *juche* that existed in feudal Korea was collective rather than individual—based first on the entire family, and then on the community.

But because of the restrictions on individual self-reliance throughout Korean history, this was one of the motivations and desires that erupted with extraordinary energy when the people were finally freed from governmental and Confucian bonds.

Since the 1960s, Koreans have strived with amazing industry to become self-reliant through education and work. On the business side, corporations expanded into virtually every facet of production and marketing in order to be self-sufficient—a move that worked like a miracle for several decades, but became a serious handicap when the huge conglomerates began to face stiff competition from abroad.

The most extreme example of *juche* probably occurred in North Korea, where the communist oriented founder Kim Il Sung made a three-pronged approach to *juche* the foundation of the economy. His whole political philosophy was based on independence, self-sufficiency and self-defense—an approach that doomed the people of North Korea to a level of poverty and suffering rare in the world today.

Juche as practiced in South Korea today—an obsession with getting an education and working with extraordinary energy to achieve a higher standard of living—remains a positive force that continues to energize the people and the government, and contributes to the goals of foreign companies doing business with and in Korea.

CHAPTER THREE

Korean Business Culture Today

The Blurring of Morality

The business environment in a very small country with a large popula-tion like Korea is intensely competitive, not only in regard to the best workers and professionals, but also for the allocation of space, licenses and other factors making up a sophisticated business structure. Since this competitive factor is combined with a very personal approach to busi-ness, the whole business environment is susceptible to what interna-tional consultant Song-Hyon Jang calls "irregular practices."

Jang says the extraordinary degree of competition and the personal nature of business in Korea has resulted in a mentality in which the end justifies the means, and that the moral implications of much of the busi-ness behavior in Korea today are blurred.

It is especially difficult for the newly arrived Western businessperson to function effectively in Korea because of the emotional, sensitive and shifting nature of the business environment. The best possible approach is for the newcomer to enlist the aid of an experienced local consultant and go-between who is a respected and influential part of the business community, and can manipulate his way through the maze of personal relationships involved in day-to-day business affairs.

This local representative may be an agent, a joint-venture partner, a broker or a consultant, but he must be someone in whom the inexperi-enced foreign businessperson can put complete faith to say and do the rights things on his behalf. Otherwise, the results can be disastrous.

Another factor continuously emphasized by such knowledgeable consultants as S. H. Jang is the importance of public image to the for-eign company. "Foreign businesspeople should give prominent consider ation to the public image of their company. Many hurdles can be surmounted if the public relations of a corporation are effective in developing a strong and favorable image," Jang said.

As is so often the case in foreign ventures by American companies, the larger the company, the more difficult it seems for it to make adaptations to fit into the Korean political and business environment. One veteran observer said that American bankers in Korea were the most rigid and inflexible of all. "You can recognize them on the street," he said. "Their inflexibility causes them so many problems it is unbelievable, and yet they persist."

Manners as Morality

Traditionally in Korea, the officially prescribed *taedo* (tay-doh), or manners, were equated with morality. Those who conducted themselves in the manner mandated by the Confucian oriented government were regarded as upright, fine people, while those who failed to follow the prescribed etiquette were regarded as immoral and subject to a variety of official and social sanctions.

The morality of individual Koreans was visible for all to see. Failure to behave in the prescribed manner was so glaring that even the smallest deviation from the correct form and tone was immediately obvious.

This kind of morality system—as opposed to the Western kind that is mostly based on an invisible internal standard—made Koreans among the best behaved of all people.

While present-day Koreans are far less manner-bound than previous generations, an impressive level of traditional etiquette is still alive and well, and distinguishes Koreans from Americans and other Westerners who are much more informal in their behavior.

Korean etiquette also has a powerful influence on foreigners who take up residence in the country. It affects their thinking as well as their behavior. Some make a conscious effort to adopt Korean manners; in others the process is unconscious.

Foreigners should keep in mind that being able to act like a Korean, including speaking the language well, is not always an advantage.

Koreans tend to treat Korean-acting foreigners like they treat other Koreans—which can range from being rude to ignoring them when there is no established relationship.

It is far more advantageous to remain in the "guest category," even if you know the etiquette and language, and benefit from the deeply entrenched custom of Koreans to treat all foreigners like guests no matter how long they may have been in the country.

Circumstantial Ethics

In traditional Korean culture, *todok* (toh-dohk), or ethics, was an etiquette thing and not a clearly defined set of principles that distinguished between right and wrong in the Western sense.

There were, of course, ethics in feudal Korea. But rather than being universal principles of conduct, they consisted of the Confucian oriented rules of behavior prescribed by the government for a hierarchically structured society—designed to be perfectly harmonious by denying people the right to think and act on their own.

In other words, Korean *todok* was a personalized set of circumstantial rules that applied to individuals in relation to their families, kin, friends, neighbors and the government—rules designed to prevent any kind of behavior that would result in disharmony and threaten the government.

In this context, all emotional expression was minutely controlled. Love in particular, was taboo because it invariably leads to emotional behavior that cannot be predicted or controlled.

Because *todok* forbid individual thinking and acting, it resulted in Korean society remaining caught in a virtual time warp for several hundred years. Almost nothing changed from the early decades of the Choson dynasty founded in 1392, until the 1890s.

With the introduction of democracy and Western-style capitalism into Korea in the middle of the 20th century, the imagination and inherent talents of Koreans were unleashed for the first time in the history of the country—with results that are obvious to the world.

But the age-old Korean system of circumstantial morality has not disappeared. In fact, as long as there is significant tolerance for a certain level of arbitrary, unfair and unjust behavior, it can be a major advantage for an individual, a company or a country to adjust morality to fit the circumstances—as was dramatically demonstrated in the recent history of Japan and China.

Foreign businesspeople dealing with Korea generally have no problem recognizing when they are presented with a *todok* situation. The best recourse is to diplomatically, clearly and succinctly point out the differences between the Korean scenario and reality, sit back or step back, and wait patiently for the other side to adjust their position.

Repeating yourself hardly ever helps and often harms, especially since there is a tendency to compromise a bit with each repetition.

The Perils of *Pipyong*

Pipyong (peep-yohng) means criticism, and refers to one of the most sensitive areas of the Korean character. Until the feudal system really began to come apart in the 1960s, superiors could humiliate and criticize inferiors, but it was strictly taboo for an inferior to criticize a superior.

This system naturally helped to perpetuate the inferior-superior hierarchical form of Korean society, the corruption that existed on every level of government and the ineptitude of many officials. It also helped to sustain one of the greatest emotional, spiritual and intellectual burdens ordinary Koreans were forced to live with for centuries.

The higher ranking an individual, the more immune he was to criticism, and there were severe sanctions against anyone breaking this taboo. Interestingly, until recent times, artists and writers were included among those who were not to be criticized because it was felt that any criticism would result in them giving up in their efforts to achieve perfection in their work.

Pipyong is no longer officially taboo in Korea. In the political area, the volume and vehemence of criticism heaped on government offices from the top down, is unbounded. In commercial enterprises however, it is still uncommon for inferiors to criticize their superiors.

But in some companies, a management technique is for managers and executives to publicly criticize individually and in groups, employees who have made mistakes in the strongest possible terms—the rationale being that such severe public reprimands will make them more productive by redoubling their efforts and avoiding mistakes in the future. This is pure Confucian psychology. It obviously works in Korean settings, but foreign managers in Korea are strongly advised against using the technique. Employees will take it from Korean bosses but not from foreign bosses.

Foreign managers in Korea should exercise great care in ensuring that any criticisms they make are done in strict privacy. In pep talks to groups, foreign managers may however, safely express dissatisfaction with overall performance in diplomatic, general terms, and include themselves in the blame and need for improvement.

The Ethics of Revenge

One of the legacies of feudal Korea that has survived in watered down form, is the cultural—and human—compulsion to take revenge when one is wronged.

The traditional etiquette and ethics of premodern Korea was such that the people became exceedingly sensitive to any behavior that shamed them or put them in a bad light—a situation that could only be wiped clean by *poksu* (pohk-suu), or revenge, of some kind.

Severe competition between families, communities, clans and government agencies—endemic during Korea's long feudal age—was the cause for much of the revenge factor in Korean society.

Most present-day Koreans are no longer as thin-skinned as their ancestors but *poksu* and *moryak* (moh-r'yahk) or revenge plot, are still something that people have to be aware of and concerned about, especially foreigners, who may unintentionally shame or insult someone.

Among the situations in foreign owned and managed companies in Korea that can result in acts of revenge against the foreigners concerned is if their attitude and behavior is perceived as arrogant, if they appear to be incompetent and yet insist on doing things their way, blaming their employees for failures, and not being sensitive and responsive to the class and competency differences in their staff.

In worst-case scenarios, aggressive individuals have been known to undermine the efforts of their foreign bosses in a concerted effort to get them removed, in order to take their places. These ploys are likely to work because in the Korean cultural context, strong, aggressive individuals invariably attract followers.

Here again, the only recourse for foreign managers in Korea is to attempt to be totally frank and open with employees, make sure that the lines of communication are always open, never show favoritism to anyone (such as those who speak English or very attractive females). In larger operations, this is another occasion when having a senior Korean mentor or consultant on hand can prevent serious consequences.

The Jealousy Virus

In the Confucian concept of an ideal society, jealousy of any kind is immoral. Thus in predemocratic Korea, wives were programmed not to be jealous of their husbands, and people as a whole were enjoined against being jealous of anyone for anything.

Because there were built-in basic differences in the lifestyles of the common people and the ruling upper class, and outwardly demonstrating or voicing any envy or jealousy was an absolute taboo, most of the people seethed with repressed jealousy. Any sign of superiority in intelligence, skill or whatever, or of a family getting ahead of others in a community, was viewed with hateful spite.

This extreme form of prejudice is still visible in Korean society, and is one of the things that now motivates Koreans to better themselves so that no one can look down on them. Also on the negative side, when individuals cannot keep up with or pass others, there is a tendency for them to try to bring the others back down to their level.

Foreigners living in Korea must be sensitive to the jealousy syndrome that still impacts on Korean attitudes and behavior, and take special care not to put on superior airs. This especially applies to interacting with government officials and the treatment of employees. Behaving in a conspicuously favorable manner toward a particular employee for example, will invariably stir up jealousy among the rest of the staff.

Present-day Korean women are especially jealous when it comes to the behavior of boyfriends and husbands—a visceral reaction to the anti-jealousy taboo that still exists in the culture. And this reaction can be especially severe when the males involved are Westerners.

Honoring Superiors

In feudal Korea, people were primarily valued for their willing acceptance of all of the customs and traditions that made up the Korean way—not for their personal skills or accomplishments.

This ancient Confucian precept virtually guaranteed that any self-esteem that common people had came from absolute obedience to the cultural and political rules that applied to their social class, sex, age, order of birth, education and occupation.

With only a few exceptions, personal ambition, initiative and anything else that might disturb Confucian harmony was taboo.

One aspect of the cultural programming of common people was the concept of *chongjung* (chohng-juung), which refers to paying deferential honor to superiors. In this case, superiors included parents (especially fathers), senior members of the family, elders in general, government authorities and various spirits and gods.

While modern-day Koreans are generally more respectful than Westerners toward the same categories of people, nowadays any respect they show is by personal choice, not by government edict or custom. In fact, after more than 5,000 years of having to keep quiet and take anything their superiors and government wanted to dish out, Koreans now speak up for their rights and are as quick as any other nationality to take action when they feel they are being wronged.

Koreans today get their self-esteem from their education, skills, experience and overall ability to succeed in a dynamic society—not from being obedient drones.

In this regard, foreign businesspeople who are in positions to measure the qualifications of Koreans for employment or whatever, should be wary of basing their judgment mainly on whether or not the individuals speak English.

While most young Koreans seem to be on their way to becoming bilingual, there are many exceptionally talented older people in the country who speak little or no English, and make better employees than English speakers.

The Social Pecking Order

There is a specific pecking order among all Koreans, and until this order is established and recognized, there can be very little interaction and no harmony. Every new employee introduced into a Korean group immediately begins taking steps to find his or her place in the hierarchy. They cannot rest until this is done.

This social pecking order can cause serious problems to the foreign manager who is not aware of it or plays it down. It often happens that the newly arrived Westerner will hire someone for a managerial position simply because he speaks English or has relevant technical knowledge, without considering his educational background or the other things that determine his social position in Korean society. The unaware foreigner then hires other people who have a higher social status to work under this manager.

The friction that is likely to result from this situation can seriously affect the operation of the whole company. Experienced expatriates in Korea avoid this problem by determining the social status of prospective employees themselves, or by relying on the input of senior Korean advisors who know how the system works and how to pick the right person for the right job.

The Faction Syndrome

People raised in the Confucian sphere of Asia have a natural propensity to form factions, in whatever group or situation they are in—a response, no doubt, to the fact that behavior in Confucian societies is based on situational ethics and not logic or humane principles that treats everyone equally. Not surprisingly, p'a (ppah), or factions, have been endemic in Korea—historically known as the most Confucian of all Asian nations.

Since ancient times in Korea, factions have sprang up in virtually every group made up of more than five or six people, coalescing around the strongest or most charismatic individual on the basis of blood ties, social class, age, birthplace, school ties and finally, common goals.

Virtually all organizations in Korea—commercial enterprises, political parties and social groups—are rife with factions. The influence of factions in political circles is visible for all to see—and feel. In commercial enterprises, factional influence is generally subtle and may require a finally tuned antenna to pick up and keep track of.

However, the larger and stronger a faction is in a commercial company, the more likely its members will make less effort to stay under cover, and the more likely they are to use their weight in getting what they want.

It can be especially important for foreign managers in Korea to be aware of any factions in their enterprises because the *p'a* may be working at cross-purposes with the policies and goals of management. This is the kind of intelligence that may come from a variety of sources, from outside consultants, customers, suppliers and bankers, to employees who are not a member of any faction or are disgruntled with one and for whatever reason, decided to inform the foreign managers.

Corporations as Military Units

Unlike their neighbors, Koreans have never had a warrior mentality even though the various historical kingdoms maintained armed forces, and occasionally warred against one another. Most of these "clan wars" resulted when a particular regime, usually over a period of several hundred years, became so corrupt the people could no longer stand it, and rose up in rebellion.

But there has long been a military aspect to the Korean mindset as a result of the Confucian principles of rigid organization and discipline that prevailed for generations.

This mindset is very conspicuous in the organization and management of Korean companies, particularly large ones. In fact, one of the best ways to view and deal with a Korean corporation is to regard it as a marine division with privates, corporals, sergeants and officers, whose lives are controlled by rank and a precise protocol.

During the decades of Korea's rapid economic growth from the 1960s to the 1990s, the Korean government itself was controlled by ex-generals, and the country was basically administered more or less as a huge army. The fact that all male Koreans in good health are required to spend two to three years in military service when they are between the ages of 20 and 25 continues to condition Korean men to military discipline and to approach their goals in life with the dedication of a soldier.

The militaristic aspects of the character of Korean companies and Korean men naturally impacts on their relationships with foreign companies and foreign businesspeople, and must be taken into account when dealing with them.

The Rank-Based Society

Like their military counterparts, Koreans are especially sensitive to *chiwi* (chee-wee), or rank. It is very important for foreign businesspeople and others to be aware of this cultural factor, and to use it properly in establishing and sustaining goodwill and good working relationships in Korea.

The rank-consciousness of Koreans has a very long history, going back to the emergence of the first clans—and then further institutionalized and ritualized by the infusion of Confucian principles some 2,000 years ago. It continues today.

You might say that Koreans love titles and the pomp and pageantry that is associated with high rank, because for many generations the only people who counted were those with titles. Titles were a major power symbol in Korea, and it was necessary to treat those with titles with extraordinary respect.

Foreign businesspeople who want to improve their chances of developing and keeping good relations with Koreans should make a point of learning their titles and thereafter, using them with and without the names of the individuals.

The rationale for using titles in addressing Korean businesspeople goes well beyond adhering to deeply entrenched etiquette. Over half of all Koreans have only six family names. In a small office, as many as half if not more of the staff, may have the same family name.

Fortunately for foreigners who do not speak Korean and have difficulty remembering titles, it is becoming more and more acceptable to address most people with the English titles of Miss, Mrs. and Mr.

However, if the individual concerned has a doctorate, in any field, it would be a serious blunder to address him or her as Miss, Mrs. or Mr. Doctor, or *paksa* (pahk-sah), the title used for anyone with a Ph.D., should be used.

Rank Has Its Privileges

Koreans have been conditioned for centuries to exist in a hierarchical society divided from top to bottom into carefully prescribed ranks, with each rank having specific kinds of acceptable behavior. This system has been greatly diluted in recent decades, but is still of vital importance in the lives of Koreans and to foreigners who do business with Koreans.

In addition to prescribed rules of etiquette within social classes, there is a prescribed form of behavior that is acceptable among the classes. Generally speaking, people in the upper classes prefer to avoid direct contact with those who are two or more grades below them, to make sure their own status is not lowered.

Business executives in particular, are sensitive about their titles and rank, and go to relative extremes to maintain their positions. They take special care not to lower their own status or raise the level of someone below them (by dealing with them on an equal basis).

Foreign businesspeople, not being members of Korean society, are normally given the "honorary" status of members of the upper-middle class. Their rank in their company and the rank and image of their company are the next most important factors in their status in Korea.

The higher their titles and the larger and better known their companies, the more prestige they enjoy. Because of the importance of social position and rank, and the necessity of knowing and following the etiquette that is appropriate for each level, Koreans are obliged to determine these factors as quickly as possible when they meet someone new.

The newly arrived foreign businessperson can greatly speed up the process of getting acquainted and establishing proper relations with his Korean counterparts, government officials and others by including his pedigree (important details about the size and sales of his company if it is not well known, the college or university he attended, including any upper-class Korean friends or contacts he might have) in his introduction of himself.

The Military Factor in Business

The military is a conspicuous aspect of life in Korea, with significant influence in politics, education, the private industry and society in general, just as it was during the country's long feudal dynasties.

Because of the ongoing threat from communist North Korea, the ROK has been on a high military alert status since the ending of the Korean War in 1953. All eligible males must register for the draft and with few exceptions, undergo military training and spend time in the reserves. Government regulations about military service are rigorously enforced. The government will not hire adult males who have not completed their military training. They may also be denied the right to obtain a passport and travel abroad.

The military training system is very thorough and tough, with strict discipline that later carries over into civilian life. There is great prestige in being selected for schooling at a military academy and going on to a career as a military officer. Those who succeed in reaching the higher ranks are invariably assured of equally prestigious positions in government or the private industry after they retire.

Most foreign businesses in the ROK accommodate themselves to this situation and attempt to see the positive side. Generally speaking, the foreign business community supports the position of the government that North Korea poses a direct military threat to the ROK. There is also a general consensus that the militaristic bent of Koreans has been a major contributing factor in the economic advances made by the ROK since the 1960s. The reference here, of course, is to the fact that Korean companies and the various government agencies marshal and manage their manpower very much like military organizations, and plot their strategies and tactics with the precision and purpose that is characteristic of military campaigns. In return, they also demand the same kind of loyalty, commitment and sacrifices that are typical of the military in do-or-die situations.

Cold Calls are Out

In earlier decades, Western businesspeople visiting Korea could ignore etiquette and make cold calls on Korean companies—first because Koreans were exceedingly anxious to make contact with foreign companies and would ignore their own ethics, and second because of a strong desire to be accommodating and hospitable to visiting foreigners.

Times have now changed, especially when it comes to large corporations. Foreigners who visit these companies without appointments may be received politely, but not necessarily by the one they want to see. It is now very important if not absolutely essential, that you have an appointment with the individual you want to meet. If you want to make any progress at all in developing a relationship, it is also vital that you make sure the individual concerned has received well in advance, a substantial amount of information about your company and yourself.

There are, of course, exceptions to these general rules and customs. Younger Korean managers and executives who have been educated abroad and absorbed Western business etiquette can often be reached by email or phone, and may agree to an appointment on short notice.

Appointments and Meetings

The pace of businesspeople in Korea might be equated with a dead run, and the higher ranking the manager or executive, the busier their schedules. Promptness is essential.

The best times for business meetings are usually 10 a.m. to 12 p.m. and 2 p.m. to 3 p.m. Business dinners are common. Mid-day meetings also take place in hotel coffee shops and restaurants. Business breakfasts are also becoming common among the international crowd.

Korean businesspeople generally take their vacations from mid-July to mid-August. Other inconvenient appointment times include early October (a time of many holidays) and Christmas time. Typical business hours are 9 a.m. to 5 p.m., Monday through Friday, and 9 a.m. to 1 p.m. on Saturday.

When entering a group meeting, the senior member of a party typically enters the conference room first, followed by the next highest ranking person, and so on. When greeting business contingents, Koreans line up in the order of their rank.

Office Call Protocol

Office calls in Korea should be treated as formal affairs, especially if you are visiting a company for the first time. It is not only polite but expeditious to make the appointment well in advance, and advise the people you want to see what you want to talk about. Koreans are reluctant to say no directly and do not like to appear uncooperative or unresponsive, with the result that the inexperienced foreign businessperson can waste a lot of time making presentations to a company that has absolutely no interest in his idea or project because they may not come out and say so.

One approach is to write to the company well in advance, providing as much details as possible about your project, thereby giving the appropriate people in the company time to discuss your proposal and at least make a preliminary decision about whether or not they want to pursue it. Companies with no interest in your project will generally eliminate themselves with a written response or by not responding at all.

Another approach—and often the best one—is to seek the assistance of a local go-between or consultant who can sound the company out on your behalf.

A significant percentage of all new business relationships in Korea begin with personal connections. The first step in approaching a company is to line up these personal contacts. At present, high-level government officials are among the most effective contacts the businessperson in Korea can have. If you can get the personal backing of an important ministry official, it will open many business doors.

At the same time, Koreans, including government bureaucrats, often do not dispense favors without expecting something in return. This something can range from an enhancement of their image to an indirect participation in the venture being proposed. These matters are usually very subtle and often require the sensitive antennae of an experienced Korean to properly execute—particularly so if you cannot communicate fluently with the official concerned.

If you do bring in a local consultant or agent, you have, of course, added another layer to whatever relationship might develop between you and your target company.

Dressing for Business

During Korea's long feudal era under the Choson dynasty, the materials, style and quality of the clothing worn by the people were determined by the government based on class and occupation. This custom made all Koreans extraordinarily sensitive to wearing apparel, and its influence continues to be conspicuously discernible in present-day Korea.

Conservative suits, shirts and ties are so much a part of the persona of Korean businesspeople that one wag noted that all male Koreans were born already dressed in three-piece suits. The conservatism that has long distinguished the dressing of Korean office workers is not as strict as it was in the 1990s, but on the average they are more sedate than their Western counterparts.

This does not mean that Western businesspeople should follow suit. But overly loud suits, shirts and ties are taken as a lack of cultural refinement and therefore do not reflect well on the wearer.

Office women in Korea are as stylish, if not more so, than their most sophisticated counterparts in London, New York, Paris or Tokyo—but on the conservative side as far as colors and cut are concerned. Skirts, blouses and suits are the norm. Pants and pantsuits for women are gradually gaining acceptance.

Sleeveless tops and miniskirts remain taboo in business settings. In many homes and restaurants, diners sit on the floor at low tables, making both miniskirts and tight skirts incompatible.

The Dual Role of Name Cards

Name cards are a vital part of doing business in Korea, not only as a means of identifying individuals by their companies and positions, but also to help distinguish between the vast number of people in the country who have the same last name. There are only seven family names among over half of the population of the country. (See *Song*).

In addition to their practical use in identifying individuals, name cards also play a significant role in helping to establish the social status of each individual and subsequently, the level of language and other etiquette that is an integral part of the social system.

The formal way to present a name card is with both hands and a slight bow, giving your name at the same time. As the power of old etiquette weakens and people become more informal in their behavior, presenting a card with the right hand is becoming common. However, using the left hand to present a card or anything else, remains impolite.

Name cards should be bilingual, not only because it is the professional thing to do but also as a courtesy to demonstrate respect for Korea and Korean culture, and as a sign that the individual is serious about doing business in Korea. Visiting businesspeople should of course, make sure they are well supplied with bilingual name cards, as it is common to go through 50 or more in one day.

If you are seated at a table when you receive someone's card, it is both customary and practical to lay it on the table in front of you so you can read the name and title during the following conversation.

Writing on someone's name card while still in their presence is still considered a no-no by some, but you can certainly do it later to help you recall the individual.

The Use of First Names

The use of first names is still not common among Korean businesspeople and adults in general. (At one time in Korean history, one's first name was kept secret. Even saying it out loud was taboo.)

Foreign businesspeople who have developed close, personal relationships with their Korean counterparts and use their first names in informal situations, should never address them by their first names at meetings or in other group or formal situations.

When speaking in English, the accepted practice in addressing people in business and formal situations is to use the common Western prefixes, Mr., Mrs. or Miss. It is also good etiquette for foreigners to use the English equivalents of the titles of ranking businesspeople and other professionals.

Gift-Giving vs. Bribery

In the Confucian sphere of Asia, gift-giving has traditionally been one of the foundations of establishing and sustaining relationships with individuals who are important in one's life—from teachers and doctors to employers, customers, suppliers and government officials.

Part of this custom evolved from ancient times, when it was customary to present gifts of food, drink and other valuables to gods and other deities to win and keep their goodwill and protection. Until money was invented, giving chiefs, priests and others something in kind was a way of paying them as well as getting their support and/or protection.

Government officials in feudal Korea had the power of life and death, so giving them *sonmul* (sohn-muhl), or gifts, became a matter of survival. Such tributes and gifts were not regarded as immoral. They were the "oil" that allowed the societies to function smoothly. Where common people were concerned, giving gifts to officials was often the only way they could get the help or services they needed.

Not surprisingly, the bounds of propriety were often exceeded, especially by well-to-do upper-class members who gave gifts to officials to repay obligations and when seeking new favors. Giving gifts in the form of tribute, primarily for protection, was also a traditional custom. From 108 BC to AD 1910, the various kingdoms on the Korean peninsula paid an annual tribute to China as a way of maintaining their independence.

During the long Choson era (1392–1910), the gift-giving custom was sorely abused by government officials and others in power who demanded what amounted to *noemul* (noh-muhl), or bribes, for their services in the guise of gifts.

Both legitimate gift-giving and out-and-out *noemul* became even more scandalous during Korea's build-up to economic prominence since 1960. In the early 1990s, the government finally enacted precise guidelines for giving gifts in an effort to cut down on the corruption engendered among government officials.

These new laws reduced but did not stop the practice of bribery in the form of gifts, and ensuring scandals engulfed even government officials on the highest levels, with two former presidents arrested and sentenced for accepting bribes.

It is now illegal to give gifts of any significance to government officials, and efforts to eliminate the practice have become stronger and more effective over the years.

Foreigners doing business in and with Korea should exercise great care to not get caught up in any gift- or favor-giving action that might be construed as *noemul*. Small, personal gifts among business friends are perfectly legal and very much appreciated by Koreans.

Foreign companies in Korea or those setting up operations in Korea, should have an anti-*noemul* statement in their corporate constitution. However, occasions may still arise in which some form of "gift-giving" may be the only solution to a problem. In which case, getting input from a senior, trusted Korean advisor on how handle the situation may be the only recourse.

Gift-giving remains an established ritual in Korea, playing a key role in creating and sustaining relationships, both in business situations and on all levels of social interaction.

Chon jimina (choan jee-me-nah), which translates more or less as "one centimeter of feelings," refers to the small gifts that Korean businesspeople customarily give to people they meet during the course of a trip, to show appreciation and express thanks for relatively small favors. It is a good practice for foreign businesspeople to emulate on their trips to Korea.

When returning home from overseas trips, it is usual for Korean businesspeople to bring gifts for their families and close work associates. It is also very common for them to buy locally famous products as gifts when they travel in Korea.

To Bow or Not to Bow

All ancient people apparently bowed down to superiors and symbols of power to demonstrate respect, inferiority, etc., but the Chinese went much further. They institutionalized and ritualized the bow, making it the formal, official way of interacting with people, from greetings and farewells, to apologies, petitions, praying, and so on.

This universalized version of the *chol* (choll), or bow, was introduced into Korea in 109 BC by the Chinese when they invaded the peninsula and more or less administered it as a province for the next 400 years. Later Korean dynasties embellished on the *chol* in a variety of ways, including the choice of language used for different occasions.

All of the guidebooks on doing business in Korea cover the role and importance of the *chol* in Korean society. The bow is still the official, formal method of greeting and leave-taking in Korean society, and there are numerous occasions when it is also appropriate behavior for Westerners—such as at formal functions, and when greeting older men and women who have not adopted Western ways.

But the Western handshake has been integrated into modern Korean society and is used when dealing with foreigners. An increasing number of Koreans of all ages now use the handshake among themselves on all but official and formal occasions.

Where foreigners are concerned, the occasion and people involved generally dictates whether one should bow or shake hands. Koreans are not bashful or reticent about sticking out their hand for a shake, so usually all the foreigner has to do is respond in kind.

Whether or not one should shake hands with a Korean is generally not a problem. Koreans are traditionally a friendly, ebullient people and unlike many Asians, often make the first move to greet a guest or new acquaintance with a good, strong handshake. Like some Latinos and Europeans, Koreans will often use both hands when they want to emphasize their goodwill, friendship or gratitude to someone.

Where bowing is concerned, there are several different kinds or grades of Korean bows, depending on the age and rank or social position of the individuals involved as well as on the circumstances of the bowing. The higher the individual, the more shallow his or her bow. Lower-ranking individuals and those expressing especially deep or sincere thanks, execute deeper bows. People seeking favors or apologizing bow lower than normal to emphasize the point.

Koreans who are used to meeting and working with foreigners generally shake hands instead of bow. The bow is not a casual gesture among Koreans. It is a very direct and conspicuous indication of their relative status—which is jealously guarded—and must therefore be performed properly to avoid giving serious offense.

When Korean businesspeople meet for the first time, they do not know how to bow to each other until their relative status is established. The first thing they usually do is exchange name cards. If this is not sufficient to clearly establish a hierarchical relationship, they may diplomatically inquire about each other's ages, schools and families.

There is a tendency for foreigners long resident in Korea to subconsciously pick up the habit of bowing, although they generally do not utilize the deep bow. They invariably learn at the same time when it is proper to bow, when a bow can be combined with a handshake, and when to only shake hands.

Newcomers who are in doubt about which is appropriate are usually safe if they combine a modest bow with a handshake with everyone except older women who have not been exposed to Westernization. One should bow to them.

Standing Up at the Right Time

It is common practice for Korean businesspeople to indicate respect for visitors to their offices by standing up. It is also regarded as impolite for lower-ranking employees to remain seated while their superior stands. This custom is reinforced by the fact that all young Korean men are required to serve a period of time in the military, where they are drilled in showing proper respect to superiors and guests, including standing up when a superior arrives on the scene.

Higher-level Korean businesspeople may not stand up when someone they do not know arrives, and this is particularly so in the case of government officials, unless informed that the visitor outranks them or is a special guest. Businesspeople and government officials may remain seated if they do not particularly want to see the visitor or do not like the visitor for any reason.

Until recent decades, women in Korea had virtually no status and were required to defer to men in virtually all circumstances. While this has changed considerably, men still take precedence over women in most common situations where Western chivalry or courtesy would put women first. Western businesspeople who demonstrate unusual courtesy to Korean women in the presence of un-Westernized Korean men may embarrass both the women and the men. The best idea in this situation is to extend basic courtesy without making a show of it.

In the rural areas of Korea, as well as in the most traditional homes and companies in Seoul and other large cities, women still take a backseat to men.

Rounds of Greetings

One of the key aspects of business relationships in Korea comes under the heading of *insa* (een-sah), which means "round of greetings." In addition to referring to the typical greetings between people on informal and social occasions, *insa* also relates to a formal obligation that businesspeople and people in general have, to visit and greet in a formal way, friends, work superiors, business and government contacts, and others who play a role in their lives.

The *insa* plays a special role in social and business affairs in Korea because it establishes the relative social position and rank of the individuals concerned, and reaffirms personal relations. Businesspeople regularly visit their key contacts to greet them formally as a way of sustaining their network of connections. A written greeting is an *insa jang*.

On the personal side, there are a number of occasions when *insa* visits are called for, including a death in the family, marriages, major holidays and other events that are important in the lives of people.

On the business front, *insa* visits to contacts in other companies and government agencies, customers and suppliers, are generally made a number of times a year. The more important the contact, the more often *insa* visits are in order. Occasions for such visits include the beginning of new projects, when an important contact gets promoted, and so on.

The most important *insa* visits occur at the close of each year, beginning around December 15, and at the beginning of each new year, between January 3rd and .5th. End-of-the-year visits are aimed at expressing appreciation to clients, customers and suppliers for their business during the year, and to request that they continue the relationship during the coming year.

Insa visits immediately following New Year's Day are even more important. These are referred to as *sebae* (say-bay), which literally means "beginning of the year bow" but is usually translated as "New Year's greeting." These are courtesy calls that people make on senior managers, directors and presidents of the companies they do business with.

The aim of the *sebae* visits is obvious—to nurture ongoing good personal relationships with key individuals to help ensure that the business relationships with their firms or agencies will continue.

Sebae visits are generally more ceremonial than end-of-the year visits and other *insa* visits during the year, with the visitors formally expressing thanks for past businesses and their sincere wishes for the continuation of the relationship during the new year.

These visits, which usually last for only a few minutes because there is often a stream of visitors calling on larger companies and more important government offices, normally include drinking toasts to each other. The events are thus festive in nature, and by mid-day, nobody is feeling any pain.

Korean companies stage their own *shimushik* (sheem-uu-sheek), or "starting business ceremony," on the first business day of the new year. These ceremonies include eating a number of special foods, drinking and lots of speeches by company executives and managers.

Foreign businesspeople stationed in Korea are well advised to follow both the *insa* and *sebae* customs.

Another custom among Korea's large corporations that foreigners need to be aware of, and emulate when the occasion arises, is known as *songbyul hoe* (sohng-buhl hoe-eh), which means "farewell party." This is a party thrown by a section or division when a member is being sent abroad on an overseas assignment.

Farewell parties are noted for numerous speeches, lots of good food and enthusiastic toasting, but they are designed to do more than just provide employees a good time at company expense. They are a way of instilling loyalty and bonding the employees.

The Korean View and Use of Contracts

The Western-style contract is still relative new to Korea. There were business arrangements of all kinds during Korea's long feudal era, many of them in writing, but they were simple agreements and documents that left the details and implementation of the contacts open so they could evolve with the changing circumstances. As in many old societies, "gentlemen's agreements" were the rule.

The emotional and friendship aspects of agreements were what made them binding. The Korean perspective was that as long as the parties to an agreement were sincere and honorable, it would be fulfilled regardless of the circumstances that might arise.

The Korean word for a Western style contract is *kyeyak* (keh-yahk), and both the word and such contracts are now common in international business relationships. But in the eyes of Koreans, a written contract is little more than a piece of paper if the parties to it are not trustworthy.

Broadly speaking, when Koreans sign contacts with their foreign counterparts, it is more of a formality indicating that they have a relationship with someone—as opposed to being an agreement that is cast in stone and to which they must abide no matter what happens.

One Korean businessperson said: "We regard contracts as general guidelines that set perimeters around which we will work."

Dyed-in-the-wool Koreans say their own *kyeyak* are based the philosophical foundation of *injong* (een-johng), or "compassion for the plight of others." They usually add, or imply, that *injong* is typically missing from Western contracts.

The already large and growing cadre of Korean businesspeople who were educated abroad and/or spent years in overseas assignments are generally at home and at ease with Western-style contracts, and when problems do develop among their stay-at-home colleagues, they can usually resolve the situation to everyone's liking.

When Koreans sign a Western contract they are putting their face, and often their fate in their companies, on the line, so it is a very serious matter. The more face they have to lose, the more likely they will adhere strictly to the contract.

While making sure that their own interests are protected, foreign businesspeople seeking to contract with Koreans obviously should bring in expert legal and cultural advisors to help make sure their contracts are acceptable to the Koreans in both a business and cultural sense.

Once large-scale contracts are worked out and signed, foreigners should follow Korean custom and mark the occasion with a celebration that includes drinks and speeches. These events traditionally end with all of the participants simultaneously raising their arms in the air and shouting "*Mansei!*" (mahn-say-ee!), which literally means "Ten thousand years!" and is the Korean equivalent of "Hip! Hip! Hooray!"

Baek ji wiim (bake jee weem), literally "trusting in white paper," is a term often used to infer that someone is doing business on the basis of nothing more solid or permanent than a piece of paper with a signature on it—which is a pretty good description of a contract. The concept derives from the fact that Koreans believe a deep personal relationship is the only proper foundation for a business relationship.

Still today, the basic Korean concept of a contract, particularly the view of government bureaucrats, differs fundamentally from the way Westerners view and use them. The typical foreign view is that once you negotiate an agreement and sign a contract, that is it; the relationship proceeds forward on mutually acceptable and solid ground. That is not the case at all in Korea. The signing of the contract is usually when trouble begins because from the very beginning, the contract is interpreted one way by the Korean side and another way by the foreign side. Generally speaking, Koreans sign contracts with foreign businesspeople to get the relationship started officially.

Thereafter, everything is subject to change and negotiation. Koreans do not regard the provisions of contracts as written in stone or as the fundamental basis of a business relationship. They regard the personal relationship and the desire for mutual benefits as the foundation of any business arrangement. A contract is essentially nothing more than a symbol of this relationship.

In the context of Korean thought, contractual obligations must change in the same way that business conditions and political situations change, in order for the relationship to be kept current—from their viewpoint, of course.

Viewed as personal agreements rather than immutable laws, the terms of a particular contract practically go out the door when the signers or the managers of a contract change. From this point, any contract is subject to the interpretations and expectations of the new managers, who devise a new set of unwritten terms to govern the relationship with the other party—and often implement these changes without informing the other side.

This is a vital difference in the concept of a contract that the foreign businessperson must understand. The essence is that when a Korean executive signs a contract with a foreign company, he is not necessarily obligating his own corporation to uphold the provisions of that contract—the corporation may not accept the obligation if it has any reason not do so. It may be regarded as a personal matter between the managers who negotiated and signed the contract, and the foreign party.

The sanctity of contracts is even less assured where government officials are concerned. Not being direct parties to the agreement, they have no qualms about declaring any contract they do not like as no longer appropriate and needing renegotiation (so as to be more favorable to the Korean side), or null and void, eliminating the responsibility of the Korean party to the contract. Since government bureaucrats are shifted around regularly (often on an annual basis), contracts between Korean and foreign businesspeople are constantly coming up for review by people who know nothing at all about them but who have the power to require that they be altered or scrapped. Incoming bureaucrats frequently feel compelled to demonstrate their efficiency and patriotism by questioning relationships between Korean and foreign companies, and ordering significant changes in their contractual arrangements.

Not all the contractual problems between Korean and Western companies is on the Korean side. Western companies too, frequently play musical chairs with their top personnel in Korea, thus breaking the personal relationships that foreign managers have established with their Korean counterparts, and making it necessary for their replacements to virtually start over in developing new ties for their companies. If these transitions are not handled thoughtfully and carefully over a period of time (and many of them are not), the switch in personnel gives the Korean side an opening to make unilateral, fundamental changes in the terms of the relationship.

It is especially important for any contract with a Korean company to be as clear, comprehensive and yet as flexible as possible. A major challenge is to anticipate changes that are likely to occur that would affect the operation of the agreement, and to make sure they are covered in the contract. Again, a shift in the managers involved in implementing a contract can affect its status.

Basically, the contract represents the intentions and understandings of the two participants at the time of signing, and if these are clear and complete, you are off to the best possible start. One problem is making sure that both sides do indeed understand what the other is saying, and are in fact agreeing to that. This may entail a great deal of extra effort in bridging the cultural differences, overcoming communications problems and really getting down to the "facts."

There is always the possibility that both sides will agree to things they really do not like just to get the contract signed, intending to deal with the issue later. This especially applies to the Korean side, and it behooves the foreign participant to make a special and patient effort to draw out the true feelings and intentions of the Korean partners.

The main thing once a contract is signed, is to maintain an ongoing dialogue with your Korean counterparts so that you can stay updated on their thinking and make the adjustments invariably necessary to keep the relationship on an even course. This is often the area in which the Western partner fails, because it requires a conscious commitment—that is time- and energy-consuming (and often costly)—to adequately nurture the relationship.

The Korean Government has attempted to address the differing cultural view of contracts by creating "model" contracts for licensing technology and other business arrangements. Both parties to such contracts must be assured that the obligations spelled out are fully understood.

Big Foreign Company Myopia

It seems that the bigger the foreign company, the more likely it is to get into trouble in Korea in both negotiating and nurturing contracts. One typical classic example involved Chrysler's famous Lee Iacocca and his top people who came to Seoul several times, made no effort at all to take advantage of the accumulated experience and wisdom of the American Chamber of Commerce in Korea (AmCham) in Seoul, and wasted a lot of time and money.

The Chrysler people spent a lot of time trying to talk Samsung, the electronics manufacturer, into going into the production of automobiles. There were already four automobile manufacturers in Korea at that time and there was no way the government was going to let a fifth company enter the field.

Samsung wouldn't let on that what Chrysler wanted was impossible because it hoped the government would make an exception of its policy and let them do it. Chrysler is said to have spent millions before they gave up, and went with Hyundai.

If the Chrysler people had had the common sense to visit Amcham, they could have learned this lesson for nothing, and saved a great deal of time, frustration and ill will. Said a local businessperson: "It was incredible that they didn't talk to a single person in Seoul to get their advice or help."

Eventually, of course, Chrysler did work out an agreement with Samsung to provide them with auto parts, but it was a very long and expensive way of developing the relationship.

Since then, a number of other American companies have gotten themselves into situations in which they were pitting their reputation and way against the Korean government or against the Korean way of doing things. This is a no-win situation and should be avoided.

Major Problem Areas

Working-level employees in Korea's government agencies and ministries do not always approve of policies advocated and announced by senior ministry officials. These officials have the power to delay or stop completely any application that comes to them, and often do so without any apparent reason for their actions.

There are also many "unpublished rules" regarding the government's approval process in any new venture. The applicant too often finds out about these internal guidelines, working rules and regulations only after applying for approval of a project.

Of course, this problem can be greatly reduced if the foreign businessperson enlists the advice of attorneys and consultants in Seoul who specialize in dealing with the appropriate government offices.

Lower-level civil servants who are responsible for the administration of the laws governing foreign investment and operation often have little if any international experience, resulting in communication problems, delays and sometimes, serious misunderstandings.

The best approach in this situation is to be very patient and helpful, and to maintain a very humble attitude to avoid rubbing the officials the wrong way. Dealing through an experienced troubleshooter, who usually already knows the officials and can anticipate their reactions and needs, can also, of course, be of significant help.

Another problem facing foreign companies in Korea are the extraordinary demands made by the government and numerous associations and charities on foreign companies for donations.

While such donations are ostensibly voluntary, when the request comes from an official in a powerful agency or ministry, it can be difficult—and may be unwise—to refuse.

Here again, a very astute local go-between who has a wide network of contacts is often needed to advise the foreign businessperson when he can safely ignore an unreasonable request for a donation.

Amcham members agree that one of the main challenges facing a foreign company wanting to establish a joint-venture operation in Korea is selecting the best possible partner. It used to be that members of the large business/industrial combines called *chaebols* generally made the best joint-venture partners because of the influence they had with the appropriate government ministries. Now, there are occasions when it can be a handicap instead of a help to join up with a *chaebol* member because the government's policy is to favor medium-sized and smaller firms over the giants.

Another usually surprising problem in tying up with one of the more successful Korean corporations, is that making huge profits is still basically regarded as immoral in the context of Korean values, so any foreign company that aligns itself with a Korean company that is conspicuous for its profits is liable to fall victim to some of the opprobrium felt toward the Korean partner.

Finally, the bigger and more successful the Korean partner, the more likely it is to insist on running the joint venture its way, regardless of what the foreign partner thinks is best.

This may work fine as long as the policies and practices of the Korean partner result in the kind of success the foreign partner is seeking. When it doesn't work out that way, the foreign partner has very little recourse.

Conflicting Goals

Joint-venture operations in Korea are subject to a great many clearly defined cultural strains that put an exceptional burden on the foreign side. One of the most important of these potential problem areas is basic conflict between the goals of the two parties.

The primary purpose of the foreign partner is to make a profit and remit dividends outside of Korea. The chief aim of the Korean partner is generally to realize company growth and make an overall contribution to the Korean economy and society at large.

Since both of these positions are virtually absolute and opposite, the only sensible recourse is for the foreign partner to be very much aware of this fundamental conflict, discuss it at length during the early stages of the formation of the joint venture, and attempt to reach a mutually acceptable agreement, in writing, on handling this important part of the business relationship.

Playing Games with the Books

There is a strong tendency for Korean companies, especially those sponsored by the government, to use "flexible" accounting practices to avoid showing a loss at the end of the year. The main reason for this creative bookkeeping where government-sponsored enterprises are concerned, is to prevent the ministry involved from investigating the company and possibly closing it down, replacing the management or publicly criticizing the management, which would harm the image of the company as well as the individual executives.

When this happens in privately owned companies, it is generally to make the company look in better shape, to save face and to avoid loss of confidence on the part of suppliers or customers. The foreign businessperson looking for an agent or partner in Korea is cautioned to do a thorough financial check before making any final decisions. Otherwise, what he sees may not be what he gets.

Privacy Korean-Style

The concept of privacy within a company is very weak in Korea. Koreans tend to assume that any matter or information that concerns the company also concerns them, and it is difficult to keep anything confidential or limited to the knowledge of an individual. Attempts to keep things from employees of a company are likely to be regarded as distrust or arrogance.

This often calls for deft diplomacy in dealing with managers and others on an internal as well as an external basis. It is especially important to avoid appearing unfair to any individual, which includes upsetting his sense of status in relation to his coworkers. There is generally no problem in protecting company confidentiality as far as outsiders are concerned, and Koreans are very sensitive about their own privacy outside the company.

There have been instances in the past, of secretaries of foreign business managers in Korea gathering up the company files and taking them to a Korean company to be copied. The moral of this story is that foreign managers should take every measure possible to ensure that their secretaries are loyal.

Working for a Boss, Not a Company

It has often been said of Koreans that, unlike the Japanese, they work for a boss instead of a company. The inference is that Koreans identify themselves intimately with the individuals they work for because it is more natural and easier for them to be loyal to an individual than to a faceless company. This means that the relationship between managers and employees is of vital importance. It also means that the foreign employer or boss in Korea must bear the responsibility of establishing and maintaining a relationship of integrity and trust between himself and his Korean employees.

It is also noted that honor and integrity among Koreans tends to be reserved for those they know, respect, trust and have an ongoing relationship with. If these conditions do not exist, the same sources say Koreans will readily sign a contract they know they are not going to keep, and will take whatever advantage presents itself.

Female Employees

The long Korean traditions of men and women virtually living in separate worlds—in their personal lives as well as work—is still an important factor in the hiring and use of female employees. Because of the lingering Confucian attitudes of the past, there is a large and growing pool of well-educated and talented young Korean women who cannot find jobs in Korean companies that befit their knowledge and ambitions.

More and more of these young women are finding employment with foreign companies, where their extraordinary energy, goodwill and talents are welcomed. Experienced foreign businesspeople resident in Korea warn, however, that using female employees as interpreters or as representatives when dealing with government officials in particular, and with senior Korean businesspeople, can cause serious problems.

The traditional male attitudes towards women in Korea are changing at what amounts to a rapid pace, but such deeply ingrained cultural concepts and customs are impossible to erase in just one or two generations. Foreign businesspeople operating in Korea should be aware of this sensitive situation and restrain their impulse to "force" their female employees on government officials or others who strongly resent this change in cultural values and do not accept it.

Although female employees are valuable assets to foreign companies in Korea, generally speaking, the "face" that the company presents to the outside must be male to ensure acceptance and cooperation.

This said, there are a growing number of small- and medium-sized companies in Korea that were founded by women and are primarily managed by women; some of them extraordinarily successful.

Women and Male Chauvinism

The pressure for Korean wives to have sons took a frightening turn in the 1970s when the amniotic fluid test used to determine the sex of unborn children was introduced. Abortions of female fetuses rose dramatically. In 1980, a more accurate and inexpensive method was introduced, and the number of abortions went even higher.

Mothers-in-law were said to be responsible for the sex tests and the decisions for aborting so many female fetuses. Male chauvinism is still a potent force in the lives of all Koreans, but Korean women are not passive vassals content to be the playthings of men. Not by any measure.

Virtually every foreigner with any experience in Korea will tell you that Korean women are stronger than the men, cleverer than the men, more dependable and more diplomatic (the latter because whatever they do publicly has to make men look good).

However, because of the strong chauvinist character of Korean males, there are few Korean women in management or other positions of public power. Those few who are in positions in which they direct males, no matter how low the level of activity, must be very careful not to upset the ego of the males. Often, the power that the females have comes from a high social position rather than from an occupational or professional position.

However, as the modern Korean women gain more personal economic security and free time, they too, began going after what they want with extraordinary passion. "They are pulling themselves up by their girdle-straps," said one veteran foreign resident and successful businesswoman in Korea.

As part of their concern for face and feelings, Koreans make great use of *chansa* (chahn-sah), or compliments, but the custom is chauvinistic in that older men do not customarily compliment women.

It is thus advisable for foreign men in Korea to be mindful of this custom in case they are tempted to conspicuously praise the looks, dress or accomplishments of Korean women in the presence of Korean men.

The Great Walls of Korea

There are a number of specific handicaps in doing business in Korea that stemmed from the Koreans' fear of excessive foreign influence and a deep-seated nationalism.

This strong nationalism plays a vital role in the success or failure of foreign companies in Korea. It is most often expressed in a negative way in regard to official government policies. Lower bureaucrats who believe that a stated government policy is bad for Korea (or a Korean company) will go to extraordinary lengths to prevent the policy or the action from being carried out.

Foreign businesspeople must learn how to deal with these problems by utilizing a variety of techniques, from enlisting the aid of influential Korean advisors or go-betweens to going to extraordinary lengths to develop close personal relationships with Koreans in the important ministries and agencies.

Another cultural factor that acts as a wall in doing business in Korea is the inferior-superior structure of Korean society. The vertical arrangements in all organizations tend to be exclusive and fiercely competitive, making it difficult or impossible for people in these vertical entities to communicate and cooperate with each other. This often results in irrational and irritating delays in any dealings, particularly those involving the government.

Disobeying Laws

Koreans are still getting used to obeying *pop* (pope), laws, that are designed to control their behavior in a democratic society in which they have free will. In earlier times, there were very few laws. Anything that disturbed the prescribed social system, as well as anything that irritated a superior, was wrong—and not detailing them in laws was seen as a way to deter people from doing anything not specifically approved.

Generally speaking, Koreans still do not like written laws, and do not agree with the principle of legalism, which calls for obeying the letter of the law. They prefer to conduct themselves and to settle differences in human terms, giving precedence to circumstances and human feelings.

Judges who deal only in facts and make decisions on the basis of written laws are regarded as cruel and antihuman, and unfit to be judges. This view of the law can cause problems to foreigners, especially Westerners, who have been weaned on the idea that the rule of law takes precedence over everything else.

Foreign businesspeople are thus advised to exhaust all practical and possible means of resolving disputes or other issues with their Korean counterparts before resorting to the law. Professional go-betweens are helpful in such cases because they bring a more balanced perspective to the issues and are much less likely to unfairly favor the Korean side.

Reading Each Other's *Nunchi*

Because of the minutely prescribed and structured form of social behavior that prevailed in feudal Korea for generations, the Korean national mindset and etiquette became homogenized to an extraordinary degree—to a point, in fact, that much of the communication became nonverbal. People could anticipate the actions and read the body language of others more or less like an open book.

The process of divining the intentions of others without resorting to words came to be known as *nunchi* (nuun-chee), which translates roughly as "to measure with the eye," or figuratively, "to read minds"—something that I have labeled "cultural telepathy."

While Korean culture is no longer as homogenized as it was prior to the 1960s—and is getting more varied every day—the traditional mind-set and behavioral patterns are still intact enough to impact directly on all relationships.

Foreigners in Korea typically encounter situations in which they are expected to divine the intentions of their Korean friends, co-workers, employees and others through *nunchi*, rather than detailed, explicit explanations. These situations can range from being mild inconveniences to being very serious problems that become even worse if they are not recognized and addressed.

Dr. C. Paul Dredge, a senior associate of Korean Strategy Associations, writing in *Korea Business World*, recounted a typical incident involving the foreign manager and a Korean president of a joint-venture company in Seoul. The firm's office was located in a very expensive but inconvenient location in Yoido, near the National Assembly Building. The foreign manager then found a nice suite of offices in the downtown area of Seoul, less expensive and far more convenient for both employees and visitors.

At the last moment, the Korean president refused to allow the move to take place and would not explain his reasons to the foreign manager. The situation developed into a sticky impasse that created a great deal of ill will on both sides.

The foreign manager had explained his reasons for wanting to move the office and believed his rationale had been understood and accepted by his joint-venture partner. He had therefore proceeded in good faith. The Korean president had opposed the move from the beginning, however, and had relied upon the foreigner's ability to read his *nunchi* to understand that he was firmly against the move although he had not said so directly.

The Korean president preferred the Yoido location because it was one of the most prestigious districts in the city. It gave the company "face" on the highest government and business levels and, as Dredge observed, "The Yoido location had nothing to do with rent and everything to do with where the company president wanted his car to pull up in the morning."

The president and other Korean personnel did not simply come out and tell the foreigner that there was no way they were going to move the offices because they did not want to confront him directly with their objections and cause him to lose face in a contest he could not win. They felt it was up to him to ask the right questions and "read" the right answers. In the end, as Dredge noted, both sides lost face in a classic case of failure in cross-cultural communications.

Added Dredge: "No amount of training in cross-cultural communication can prepare an expatriate manager to conduct the technical aspects of the business of his company in Korea. But adding cross-cultural sensitivity to his technical and managerial skills, and experience puts the manager and his company at a distinct advantage—in discussions of office location, in contract negotiations, in adjustment to family life in Seoul and in every other aspect of his daily activities, both professional and personal."

Learning how to communicate with Koreans via *nunchi* is not something that comes easily or quickly. In addition to a good command of the Korean language, one has to become sensitized to every nuance of the verbal and body languages, and know how to interpret them. This means that the average foreign businessperson in Korea needs to have access to advice from a very loyal and very experienced Korean to act as his or her "cultural telepathy" interpreter.

Being skilled at *nunchi* is one of the most important business and social assets a person can have. Such people are highly valued because they are the ones who help keep a workplace peaceful and productive.

Of course, this facet of Korean culture puts foreigners at a decided disadvantage—unless they are bilingual and bicultural. Not being able to tune into the cultural channel that reveals the *kibun* (feelings or real intentions) of Korean employees, foreigners have to depend on help from others—usually an older and seasoned employee who is genuinely interested in and committed to the welfare and success of the individual foreigner and his company.

Fortunately, younger generations of Koreans, particularly those with international experience, are becoming less sensitive about keeping their *kibun* intact as they become more individualistic and self-assured.

The word itself is now heard much less often than in the past, but the feelings it refers to are still a significant part of the Korean psyche and should not be ignored.

In the past, it has most often been the Korean businessperson who learned the Westerner's ways and made adjustments to accommodate them. The advantages of inter-culture understanding accrued to him alone. In recent years, however, Korea's position as an emerging economic power has created a flow of economic activity so dynamic that the cultural accommodation of only one side of the Western-Korean partnership is no longer sufficient for either side.

Dr. Dredge says that some expatriate managers have grown tired of hearing that things are done differently in Korea, but "when they and their colleagues put forth the effort necessary to learn the fundamentals of how that is so (or to distinguish between important cultural differences and cases in which citing such differences is little more than a beginning ploy), they can use their knowledge not only to avoid making mistakes, but to gain positive management and negotiating skills."

The Role and Importance of Social Status

Social status remains a vital factor in personal and business relations in Korea. The foreign businessperson who is going to establish an office or factory in Korea must be aware of this and take it into account. To employ a Korean with a low social status as a manager—because of his English language ability, his experience or any other qualification—and expect him to be able to effectively manage employees with higher social pedigrees will usually result in problems.

Generally speaking, the higher the Korean is in the managerial hierarchy of a foreign company, the higher his social status should be to avoid undesirable repercussions from other employees. Social class in Korea is determined by several factors including ancestry, schools attended, where the individual was born and where the person presently lives. The social elite in the country is made up of people whose ancestors were high-level government officials, successful businesspeople and educators, who were born in Seoul, attended the right high schools and universities (Kyung Ki High School and Seoul National University are the highest ranking schools in the country), live in a prestigious district of Seoul and have a relative degree of family affluence.

Relationships and Connections

Among the hundreds of culturally pregnant words that are windows to the etiquette and ethics of Koreans, there are two that are especially meaningful in the business world: *yeon* (yohn) and *yonjul* (yohn-juhl). *Yeon* means "personal relationships," and *yonjul* means "personal connections"—both discussed before.

In traditional Korean society, all relations between and among people were based on and controlled by the existence, or non-existence, of a relationship—a blood tie, a school tie, a work tie, social class or some prior involvement.

Virtually all life revolved around one or more of these relationships. One simply did not go out and establish a new relationship on the spot in order to make a new friend or accomplish a goal. Relationships that were unnecessary were virtually taboo. And generally speaking, social relationships and connections did not cross class lines.

When it became desirable or necessary to form a new relationship, the only approved way was through *yonjul*, that is, connections. To repeat the nation or state analogy, establishing new business relationships required going though a kind of diplomatic procedure that included introductions and a series of formal meetings.

Korea still operates for the most part, on relationships and connections. Businesspeople spend a lot of time and money creating and sustaining relationships with other individuals in companies and with government agencies.

Foreign companies in Korea must go through the same process of developing and maintaining contacts, and some wisely identify and retain senior Korean advisors or consultants who can quickly plug them into the kind of network that is essential for success in Korea.

The dictates of *yeon* make it imperative that personal relations be established between two people before they can engage in business or interact socially. This personal relationship is established through acceptable introductions and then a number of face-to-face meetings that involve eating and drinking together, getting to know each other's personal background, and establishing common interests, trust and confidence in each other.

Because the personal relationship must precede any business dealings, it requires an investment in time, effort and money that the foreign businessperson is likely to regard as wasteful and foolish. And many, despite knowing about the requirements of *yeon* in Korea, will often ignore them and proceed as if they were in the US, where such personal requirements are minimal.

Yonjul, or connections, are something Koreans cannot do without. Virtually all areas of work and private life depend on making and maintaining networks of close personal connections. The foreign businessperson who wants to succeed in Korea must develop and nurture the same kind of networks.

The person in Korea who seems to know everybody and be able to do almost anything through his connections is said to have a *bal i nulba* (bal i nulba), meaning "wide leg," instead of a "wide face" as in Japan. Because most business within the private industry as well as with the government is based on having extensive personal contacts, the person with a "wide leg" is especially valued in Korea.

Human Harmony in Management

The Korean-Confucian concept of harmony in human relations is expressed in the word *inhwa* (een-whah). It is a concept that incorporates both loyalty on the part of employees, and maternal concern and behavior on the part of employers toward their workers.

Goldstar Inc. (which later changed its name to LG) was long regarded as the primary advocate of the *inhwa* style of management. It produced a book by that name that was used as a manual—some say "bible"—by the employees of the company. The guidelines in the manual included all of the traditional Confucian concepts of loyalty, unselfish goodwill, the maintenance of harmony in all human relations, respect for authority, plus a strong theme of Korean spirit and Korean nationalism based on some 5,000 years of historical accomplishments.

When LG established a factory in Huntsville, Alabama, the primary principles of *inhwa* were incorporated into its management philosophy, apparently with significant success.

Ties that Bind

Prior to the introduction of Western business practices in Korea, virtually all business deals were made and kept on a foundation of trust and mutual obligation—a custom that worked well because in the absence of precise laws, that was the only choice people had.

The whole framework of Korean society was, in fact, built on a foundation of *shinyong* (sheen-yohng), or trust, that was manifested in the etiquette and ethics of all relationships, beginning with the family unit and its members.

Korean sociologists have even come up with a trust scale that shows how Koreans typically categorize people. Only members of the immediate family receive 100 percent on this trust scale. Nephews and nieces came in at 99 percent; cousins at 97 percent and other relatives at 96 percent. High school classmates were rated at 97 percent, and college classmates at 85 percent. People with the same family name, as well as those with ancestral homes in the same locale, came in at 70 percent.

Other Koreans with whom one had no relationship of any kind, and were strangers, came in as low as five percent. Foreigners with whom one had no relationship came in at one percent.

Most Koreans say these assessments are too narrow, but generally speaking, they continue to be applied in most life situations, including employment decisions. Until the early 1990s, most large Korean corporations hired all of their employees from just one or two schools in order to take advantage of the built-in ties that existed among the graduates.

Given this mindset in the etiquette and ethics of Korean businesspeople, it is imperative for foreigners going into Korea to be aware of the trust factor in their hiring and in developing a circle of business and government contacts in the country.

It is highly recommended that companies planning on going into Korea begin the process of establishing a network of contacts months if not years, in advance. This can be done through embassies, chambers of commerce in Korea, banks, service clubs (Rotarian and Kiwanis), professional associations, local groups of expatriate Koreans, Koreans attending schools in the country concerned, and the foreign subsidiaries of Korean companies.

Generally speaking, it takes a minimum of three years before a newly arrived company and its managers are accepted by the world of Korean business, and then only if they are active outside of their offices and follow the rules of etiquette that are expected of all businesspeople.

The Importance of a Dignified Manner

The typical informal and often, loud and rowdy behavior of many foreigners (which unfortunately often includes Americans), can be upsetting to Koreans whose traditional etiquette is highly refined and stylized. Even the touching and backslapping behavior of ranking foreigners, done to express friendliness and goodwill, may be construed as undignified by more conservative Koreans who still live by the code of etiquette that was an integral part of their culture for some 2,000 years.

One of the main facets of this etiquette code was *wiom* (we-ohm), or dignity—a type of stylized behavior that included keeping their emotions under control, maintaining an outward calm that concealed their thoughts and protected their face, using the correct form of speech to whomever they were addressing, bowing and conforming to other types of body language mandated by the circumstances, and wearing the clothing appropriate for their class and position.

Still today, most Koreans conduct themselves with a degree of dignity that distinguishes them from other people. This is something that foreign businesspeople should be aware of and take into consideration when meeting and associating with their Korean counterparts.

Wiom and "face" are closely associated in the Korean mindset. They are especially sensitive to any remark or action that wounds their dignity (face), including such things as failure to use the title of a high-ranked individual, criticizing someone in public, or asking someone to do something that they do not feel is part of their duty, or is below them.

Traditionally, the only time Koreans dispensed with their strict code of dignity was when they were drinking at an after-hours dinner party or gathering of some kind, and basically this still holds among business associates today. At such events, Koreans expect any foreigners in the group to also drop their dignity shields and behave in an informal and sometimes rowdy and raunchy way—the latter if the gathering is in a cabaret or *kisaeng* house.

However, foreign businesspeople do not have to take a course in Korean etiquette to get by without damaging someone's dignity. It is sufficient to be reserved and polite (by standards of Western etiquette), and let their Korean counterparts set the tone.

Older Koreans who are traditional in their attitudes and behavior put great stock in *wiom* so it is especially important for one to react properly toward them—meaning politely, with studied restraint and grace. This does not mean, of course, that one should compromise on ethics or principles in acknowledging this deeply entrenched social custom.

The Decision-Making System

The traditional Korean system of decision-making is called *pummi* (poom-mee), meaning "proposal submitted for deliberation." But the system is more form than content, says Dr. Il Chung Whang, Dean of Business and Economics College, Han Yang University. Dr. Whang says the primary use of the *pummi* system is to diffuse responsibility and that its use varies greatly with the size and type of company.

Proposals are written and then circulated vertically within the company. One of the most important functions of the *pummi* system, according to Dr. Whang, is to provide documentation for company programs.

However, the smaller the company, the less likely it is to depend on the consensus approach to decision-making. In fact, it is said that in all of Korea the only company that makes a concerted effort to follow the consensus approach to management was the Daewoo group, which fell on hard times. According to this view, the chief executive officer of each of the Daewoo companies expected all decisions to be unanimous, and each saw his role as asking questions and listening.

The process of decision-making in the private industry in Korea is similar to that in American companies that practice participation management. Senior managers have the authority to, and often do, make decisions on their own—especially in the case of founder-owners. But generally speaking, there is a considerable amount of consulting among middle and upper management before major decisions are made.

This process, which is quite different from the well-known Japanese system of "bottom-up" management by consensus, still requires a considerable degree of agreement among all levels of management, and therefore takes time.

Foreigners approaching Korean companies cannot confine their dealings to one or two individuals at the top. They must also develop cooperative relationships with all the section or department heads that would be involved in their project.

Despite the surface similarities to Western management, the decision-making process within Korean companies generally cannot be rushed—with the obvious exceptions being in the "one-man" companies run by their founders or their equally strong-minded sons.

The area of decision-making in Korea that stretches the typical Western businessperson to the limits (and beyond) is government agencies and government-controlled organizations. Here, the situation is much more like it is in Japan, with a few added twists and turns that often amaze and frustrate foreigners who are not familiar with the psychology and processes that prevail in the ROK government.

Virtually every decision or action wanted from the government or a government-controlled entity must be initiated at or near the lowest level of activity, and work its way upward through the intricate, sensitive, vertically ranked departments. Because of the paranoia among government employees about being saddled with any kind of individual responsibility—and their obsession about covering every conceivable point, often from every conceivable angle—this process generally requires an inordinate amount of paperwork and redundancy that would try the soul of any but a Korean saint.

Another aspect of interpersonal relations in the structure and psychology of Korean society and business is that there is often very little communication and cooperation between vertically structured departments in a government agency or corporation. This frequently results in the outsider having to deal with different departments as if they were different agencies or companies.

Generally speaking, the Confucian values of Korean society require that all decisions take into consideration the personal feelings and harmony of the group. The manager considering a proposition must give as much thought to its effects on the harmony of the group as to its business or economic benefits to the company.

This need for maintaining harmony is sometimes so overpowering that it takes precedence over other strictly business considerations. When this happens to the unconditioned Western businessperson, he may doubt both the goodwill and intelligence of the Korean businesspeople concerned.

This same cultural component of business in Korea colors the entire management process, from the day-to-day flow of work to goal-setting and evaluation. It is an emotional and psychological aspect of business relationships in Korea that the Westerner must understand and deal with effectively to succeed.

In addition to contending with the need for group harmony, the Western businessperson in Korea must also beware of expecting any significant degree of creativity from the average Korean manager or worker. The harmony factor prevents a great deal of individual initiative that Westerners normally expect, but equally important in reducing creative thinking in Korea is the rote system of learning used in schools. Not having been encouraged or allowed to think creatively, the average Korean employee is more likely just to accept things as they are without question.

Western businesspeople with extensive experience in Korea add that Korean workers often come up with shortcuts in how to do a particular job—but often without considering the consequences, so that the final results may be undesirable. In such situations, the Westerners add, the typical Korean will say nothing about the problem and it will continue until noticed by someone else.

Tangchal yok (tahng chahl yahk), literally "power of insight," is the term used to describe the visceral feeling by which Korean businesspeople often make decisions—as opposed to using intellectual reasoning or logic. Because of the pervasive cultural conditioning Koreans undergo, they are also able to communicate to an extraordinary degree without using words, almost as if by telepathy.

Foreign businesspeople dealing with Koreans are often nonplussed by this system of decision-making and communicating, often wasting a lot of time in trying to use logic when the Korean side is seeking to develop personal rapport. Another interesting word that makes reference to the belly area is *baetchang* (bate-chahng), or "leather belly," which refers to a man who really has no assets but behaves as if he were rich.

Negotiating Korean-Style

The process of *kyosop* (k'yoh-sop), or negotiating, in Korea is naturally a microcosm of the culture in action—a culture that remains very traditional in many ways.

Koreans are tough and wily negotiators because their social experience is far more emotional and given to dramatic tactics than is common in the West. Their cultural conditioning to express themselves in vague terms and keep their real intentions hidden until the last moment is also irrational and upsetting to Westerners.

Another Korean tactic in negotiating is to swing back and forth between being confrontational and compromising—something that further upsets and imbalances Westerners who are used to a straight forward, even keel approach in their negotiations. The Korean goal tactic is to wear the other side down and achieve their goals in small increments.

Westerners generally come to a negotiating table with their presentations in order and the perimeters of their authority firmly fixed. Koreans generally come in without having settled all of the details of their position, and often have to stop the negotiations and consult with one another and others in the company. [Notwithstanding this description, Koreans point out strongly that they are generally more forthcoming and clearer than the Japanese in their negotiating style.]

Korean negotiators often switch their positions 180 degrees without any explanation for their actions—something Westerners also find unsettling. This, interestingly enough, is fairly common in all authoritarian, hierarchical societies. The rationale for this kind of behavior is that negotiators will maintain a certain position to the point where the threat of it backfiring appears imminent, and then reverse themselves as a protective measure.

This kind of behavior is difficult for Westerners to understand and accept because it often appears to be totally arbitrary and disruptive on purpose. It is arbitrary but it is also serious. The Korean negotiators are gambling that the other party will fold and they will win.

One of the explanations of this kind of behavior is the so-called "winner takes all" attitude that is common in the Confucian sphere of Asia. Once failure becomes obvious and inevitable, the losing side subordinates itself to the winner without any psychic damage, and thereafter becomes enthusiastic collaborators and supporters—a common survival technique among people whose morality has traditionally been situational rather than based on fundamental principles.

Other aspects of the Korean negotiation style: throwing in some kind of surprise that catches the other side off guard, as in a chess game, and a degree of stubbornness that verges on being, or actually is, irrational. This surprise maneuver is known as *sunsu chida* (suun-suu chee-dah), which means "first to draw," or "first to strike."

Negotiation Do's and Don'ts

Koreans are clever and forceful negotiators. They are not conditioned by any sense of fair play or of not taking advantage of a weaker adversary. They will take all they can get. There is also the very strong feeling that foreigners have so much and they have so little that it is only right that they should get more than the foreign side does out of any relationship.

One vital point the foreign businessperson should keep in mind when in Korea to negotiate any kind of arrangement, is to never let the Korean side know when you are scheduled to leave. If you do, they will invariably lead you on and wait until the last minutes or even seconds to inform you that they cannot accept your terms. This puts the foreign visitor under tremendous pressure to make last-minute concessions in order not to go home empty-handed. The same caution applies to doing business in Japan.

Typically, say old-timers, the visiting American businessperson reacts in one of two ways: he "gets hot, blows a gasket and kills the deal, or he gives in and lets the Koreans have what they want." A similar approach is often taken in labor-management negotiations, with union leaders assuming seemingly irreconcilable positions until the last few seconds of a deadline, when they will suddenly accept a compromise.

The foreign negotiator must know his own products and company, clearly how flexible he can be, and be as knowledgeable as possible about his Korean counterpart. Foreign businesspeople often negotiate deals or contracts with Korean companies without leaving their hotels, having only the name and very general information about the Korean side. Like their Japanese cousins, the Koreans negotiate in groups and are masters at wearing opponents down. The more important the relationship, the more troops the foreign businessperson should bring along.

One of the keys to successful negotiations in Korea is to know in advance exactly who you will be facing, how many people, their titles, specialties and responsibilities. Matching them with your own team is a bare minimum. The best approach is to bring in people who are senior in age, experience and authority.

When you are on Korean turf, the managers of the meeting will direct you to the side of the table reserved for guests—the one facing the door. There is, of course, the usual small talk with tea or some other soft drink served. Once the talks get underway, the Korean side will generally be aggressive and sometimes loud. They can be blunt and apparently frank. These passionate outbursts should not be taken personally. It is part of the Korean style.

You can demonstrate your own controlled passion, or let the Korean side vent itself before proceeding in a calm, collected manner. Which method works the best depends on the goals of the Korean side, how close or far apart the two sides, and often, the personality of the leading Korean at the table.

The Korean side will typically hold side discussions during the negotiating process, and will often not respond immediately to points or questions.

The Bargaining Factor in Business

Prior to the beginning of modern capitalism in Korea (which really did not take hold until well into the 20th century), prices for goods and services were generally arbitrary, depending on a variety of circumstances.

This situation, which existed from the beginning of Korean history, resulted in the people becoming skilled at *enuri* (eh-nuu-ree), or bargaining, and in bargaining becoming a national characteristic—something that people took for granted and did automatically.

Most prices are set in Korea's brick-and-mortar places today, but in street stalls and markets, *enuri* is still the order of the day. Being good at bargaining is regarded as a necessary social skill.

Not many Westerners have had more than "tourist experiences" at bargaining. They are usually not good at it, reluctant to do it and generally get taken when they try. What further disadvantages them is that the Korean approach to the process is emotional. If they encounter any kind of real resistance on the part of a potential buyer, they tend to become loud and passionate.

But these displays of passion are recognized and understood "acts" that are part of the process, and thoroughly enjoyed by the players. These sessions are described as *chugoni-batkoni* (chuu-goh-nee bath-koh-nee), or give-and-take, as well as *oksinkaksin* (ohk-sheenpkahk-sheen), or pushing back and forth.

Not surprisingly, Korean businesspeople bring their bargaining skills and techniques to the negotiating table when dealing with Westerners, who have generally been conditioned to use facts and logic to present their cases.

Foreign businesspeople should be forewarned that there will likely be a great deal of emotionally charged stagecraft in their negotiations with Koreans, and be prepared to calmly ride them out—or if they are secure in their position, throw a few emotional punches of their own.

Controlling Competition

Part of the etiquette and ethics of traditional Korea was the cultural and political imperative that kyongjaeng (k'yohng-jang), or competition, be categorized and controlled by the government and by custom, to avoid friction and maintain social harmony. This, in part, was in keeping with the Buddhist concept that competition that resulted in some people being better off than others was immoral.

This system was another of the many factors that worked to repress innovation and invention—both of which can change the competitive factor in a business—during Korea's long feudal period. This system, however, primarily applied to individuals acting on their own.

Competition between families, communities and commercial enterprises was not considered immoral as long as it was done on a group basis. And within families and other groups, individuals could and did compete fiercely.

With the end of the feudal laws controlling Korean behavior in the 20th century, Koreans took to individual competition with a focus and energy that is remarkable.

Koreans today do not like to lose or come in second in any endeavor, whether it is sports, working, entertaining or anything else. Individual Koreans see themselves as representing their immediate family, their relatives, their community and the whole nation. They are driven by a compulsion to excel and succeed.

This cultural characteristic is another of the factors that played a role in the rise of Korea to economic prominence, and continues to make Koreans among the most competitive of all workers.

Hospitality and Business

One of the most interesting—and often startling—aspects of Korea's traditional etiquette and ethics is the role of hwandae (hwahn-die), or hospitality. Koreans are among the most hospitable people on the planet, and in business situations their hospitality can be so aggressive that it surprises and sometimes shocks Western visitors.

Like most Asians and some Westerners, Koreans have traditionally marked special occasions with sumptuous meals and the uninhibited consumption of alcoholic drinks. In business situations in particular, it is customary for Koreans to lay on the *hwandae*, frequently to the point that they literally force guests to drink.

A lady of my personal acquaintance, the CEO of a medium-sized high-tech company, recently went to Seoul to meet her Korean agent. After meetings all day, the president of the agency insisted on taking her out for a barbecue beef dinner and drinks. Within a short time, he was drunk and became even more aggressive than before in trying to get her to drink, and in his comments about his marriage and sex affairs when he was away from home.

The lady was embarrassed and as the evening wore, became more and more angry. The two young male aides to the president who were with them were obviously aware that their boss was going too far, but they said nothing and did nothing. At about 2 a.m. in the morning, the lady escaped by literally crawling under the low Korean-style floor table, and running out of the restaurant.

This incident was no doubt more shocking to a lady than it would have been to a man, but it was not unusual behavior for a Korean businessman. Foreign businesspeople who do not want to over-drink or abuse themselves by staying out beyond a reasonable hour, should not hesitate to make a plausible sounding excuse or explanation to limit their drinking and end the evening at a decent hour. This is one of a growing number of occasions when not doing things the Korean way is the right way.

Foreign visitors should also keep in mind that the Western custom of "going Dutch" is alien to the traditional Korean way of thinking and behaving, especially where businesspeople are concerned. The exceptions are students and close friends who frequently go out, or stop in some place for drinks, and are not trying one-up anybody.

In the case of Korean businesspeople, politicians and the like, they gain face by acting as the host, and the more elaborate the dinner or party, the more face they gain. This often puts Western businesspeople who are on tight company budgets in a bind because they cannot match the freewheeling ways of their Korean counterparts.

Private Invitations

Koreans are enthusiastic hosts, and tend to be much more open in their relationships with foreigners than most other Asians, particularly older generation Japanese.

In Japan, people traditionally did not entertain friends in their homes—in part because their homes were small and crowded. The custom was—and generally still is—to treat friends and visitors at restaurants.

Koreans on the other hand, particularly those in the middle and upper classes, delight in inviting foreign guests to their homes for meals that are more like banquets than daily fare. Those who have traveled abroad, or are engaged in international business, take special pleasure in extending *chodai* (choh-die) or "invitations" to foreign guests.

The openness demonstrated by the custom of inviting foreign guests into their homes is one of the reasons why many foreigners find working and living in Korea more natural and more satisfying than what is generally experienced in some other Asian countries.

Business Dining

When invitations for a meal are extended to you, they should be accepted, as well as reciprocated, within a reasonable amount of time during your visit. Dinner is the largest meal of the day, and usually takes place between 6 p.m. and 8 p.m.

Entertaining frequently takes place in restaurants and coffee shops. If you are invited to a home, consider it an honor.

While it is common in other countries to extend dinner invitations to spouses, this is not the case when interacting with South Koreans. Business entertaining is only reserved for the parties directly involved in the negotiations.

The person who extends the invitation is expected to pay for the meal. In non-business situations, it is considered polite for the younger person to pay, or at least offer to pay, for an older person. Regardless, a good-natured argument over who will pay is to be expected. If you want to pay for the meal, a common tactic is to pretend to go to the washroom a little before the party ends, and pick up the tab from the cashier or server before anyone else can.

In dining, the traditional protocol is to wait for the eldest person or honored guest to start eating first.

Tipping is still not common in Korean restaurants. A service charge of 15 percent or more is automatically included in restaurant and hotel bills. However, some diners leave a tip if the service is exceptional.

Business Drinking

As in many societies, drinking alcoholic beverages in Korea was originally linked with religious rituals, apparently because it was believed that it was possible to commune more directly with the gods when in a drunken or trance-like state.

In earlier times, women were allowed to drink, but with the introduction of a more strict form of Confucianism in 1392, the role of women in society changed dramatically, and drinking was one of the many things that became taboo for the female population.

The men, on the other hand, drank during religious rituals, during festivals and "after hours" dinners or parties with male friends. Drinking became especially important to men in the highly structured and layered Korean society because that was the only time they could dispense with the restrictive interpersonal protocol that controlled their behavior at other times.

When industrialization came to Korea in the 20th century, *kyojesul* (k'yoh-jeh-suul) or business drinking, became an integral part of developing and maintaining interpersonal relationships between coworkers, suppliers and customers.

Still today, *Kyojesul* plays a key role in formal company affairs, such as celebrations to mark the end of successful meetings with outside contacts, entertaining guests, customers and government officials, in after-hours coworker sessions that are designed to build company loyalty and spirit, and to air grievances that cannot be done during working hours because of the culture of saving-facing and the powerful need to avoid hurting anyone's feelings.

Foreigners who are new to Korea may be put off by the change in Korean behavior at drinking sessions. They typically become much more aggressive in their demeanor, invariably insisting that their guests drink heartily—often to excess—and may not take "no" for an answer.

There is a ritualized etiquette in such after-hours drinking. Members of the host party, beginning with the chief host, insist on repeatedly pouring drinks for guests, even when their glasses are not empty.

Leaving your glass full to limit the volume you drink doesn't work. Host members insist that you take a drink to partially empty your glass every time they approach you—which can be every minute or so during an evening.

Aggressiveness during drinking parties is part of the effusive hospitality of Korean hospitality, but it is also derived from a desire to get one drunk to see how he or she behaves when the strict day-time rules of etiquette go by the wayside.

Most Korean businesspeople have *sulchinku* (suhl-cheen-kuu), or drinking partners, whom they meet regularly to relieve stress by getting things off their chest, and to network and get help when they need it.

This is a custom that is highly recommended for foreign businesspeople who are stationed in Korea or visit there regularly, since *sulchinku* came be invaluable sources of cultural advice and connections.

In any event, "business drinking" continues to play a key role in the etiquette and ethics of Korean businesspeople and government officials. It is an important part of the culture, and should not be ignored by foreign businesspersons.

Tangol (tahn-gole), literally a "sweet place," is a bar where a businessperson has developed a close relationship with the owner or manager and the hostesses, and is treated as a special customer. It is a place he takes new friends and clients, and where he goes when he needs to have attractive women fuss over him and make him feel good. Such bars are also called *tanga* (tahn-gah).

The practice of keeping one's own bottle at a favorite bar, called "bottle-keep" (boe-tahl-kee-puu) was introduced into Korea from Japan, but it is less common. "We drink so much there is almost never anything left in a bottle to leave at a bar," said a Korean executive, laughing.

Bangsuk ul galda (bahng-suuk ule gall-dah) literally means "to put a cushion under someone" (to make sitting more comfortable). It is used in reference to wining, dining and otherwise catering to a person you want something from—at which Koreans have a special talent.

Still today, most Korean men who do not have health problems drink, and refusing to drink without an acceptable excuse is regarded as unfriendly, if not antisocial. However, some younger Koreans are beginning to resist the pressure to drink heavily, and abstinence or moderate drinking is becoming more acceptable.

Acceptable excuses include a health problem and religious beliefs. If you do not drink, it can become awkward for you and for your Korean hosts or guests, since they will drink and have a raucous and often rowdy time, while you remain sober.

It is common for every member of a group to make the rounds, refilling the glasses of seniors and guests. In some cases, the senior Korean host will begin this process by refilling the glass of the guests in the order of their rank. The larger the group, the more people may make the rounds and the more pressure there is to drink to excess.

One approach, even if you are a non-drinker, is to take tiny sips of beer or some other relatively weak drink and then simulate the level of tipsy behavior that keeps you in tune with the group. [I have also surreptitiously dumped drinks in flowerpots.] Whatever the situation, when you do not want your glass refilled, empty it then turn it upside down on the table.

When your glass is being refilled it is polite to hold it with one hand, supporting that hand with the other hand. Another custom when individuals in a group want to demonstrate the closeness of their relationship is for two individuals to exchange drinking glasses or cups and toast each other.

When the party is in a hostess club or a karaoke bar, it almost always includes singing after everyone becomes loose. Guests are expected to sing. If you are not up to singing solo, dragging a cohort or a member of the Korean group onto the stage to sing with you is acceptable.

Singing Your Way to Success

It might seem far-fetched to Western businesspeople who have not been to Korea (or Japan) to suggest that they brush up on their singing as part of their preparations for the trip.

In fact, singing in groups and in solo performances before live audiences has been a part of the cultural tradition of Koreans since ancient times. *Norae* (noh-rye), or singing, began as part of shamanistic rituals and celebrations that required the participation of everyone.

From this very early tradition, singing became a form of folk entertainment and played an even more important role in the lives of people. Chinese travelers on the Korean peninsula in 1,000 BC reported that in a number of the tribal nations they visited, it was customary for the people to gather around open campfires in the evening and hold impromptu songfests. The Chinese visitors wrote that in one tribe, the people devoted the entire month of October to singing and dancing.

The royal courts of all of the kingdoms that later developed on the Korean peninsula maintained troupes of professional singers and dancers to entertain the royal families, ministers and state visitors. One of the primary skills of Korea's professional warrior class, which appeared during the Shilla dynasty (57 BC–AD 669), was singing and dancing.

As time passed, all Koreans began singing for the pleasure of it, and over the millennia, learning a large number of folk songs in early childhood became an integral part of growing up. Thereafter, people sang throughout their lives—at parties, at festivals and other celebrations.

The most famous of Korea's professional singers were the *kisaeng* (kee-sang), young women chosen for their beauty and taught from an early age to sing, dance, play musical instruments and provide titillating company to men (preceding Japan's more famous geisha by more than a thousand years).

In the 1890s, before the last Korean dynasty ended in 1910, there were some 10,000 *kisaeng* attached to the royal court in Seoul.

Suffice to say, singing has had a long and important role in Korean history, and continues today to be an important feature of society. Many Koreans follow the tradition of engaging in *jang ki* (jahng kee), which means "favorite technique," and refers to privately practising some skill—usually singing—so that when they can perform in public they will not embarrass themselves and will impress people.

Korea also imported the karaoke boom that started in Japan, and went one better with a proliferation of *norae bang* (noh-rye bahng) or "singing salons" that went well beyond the karaoke bars in Japan.

Businesspeople sing at dinner and drinking parties—both of which are an integral part of doing business in Korea—as well as at celebrations and other events.

Any foreign businessperson who spends three or more nights in Korea will almost invariably be invited to an evening out where singing is part of the action—and be expected to sing.

In earlier years, Koreans naturally assumed that everyone could sing, but where most Europeans and especially Americans were concerned, they soon learned better. But that hasn't stopped them. They still insist that everyone sings, and this insistence can be aggressive.

The foreign businessperson who really wants to make it in Korea will have to learn how to sing. This is a very big order for most Westerners, but it can be one of the most valuable skills one can have. Singing is an important part of the upbringing of Koreans, and is institutionalized at eating and drinking parties where businesspeople unwind, relax, enjoy themselves and do the psychic communication that is so important to their emotions, spirit, mood—and image of other people.

Foreign businesspeople are automatically expected to participate in these nighttime singing sessions and not being able or willing to join in, no matter how badly one might perform, is a serious handicap. As silly as it might seem, any foreign businessperson expecting to go to Korea should first lock himself in his bathroom (or go out in the desert, open fields or mountains) and practice belting out two or three oldies that he is at least vaguely familiar with. Being a really good singer is seen as a talent that is just as valuable as other desirable life skills—and sometimes more so, because it contributes directly to close communication and feelings of friendship and well-being.

In any event, it is the effort one puts in that counts, not the quality of the singing.

Having Fun in a *Kisaeng* House

Japan's geisha and the term geisha house are well known around the world, but what is not so well known is that Korea had *kisaeng* (the Korean equivalent of geisha), hundreds of years before the appearance of the first geisha in Japan.

Korea's *kisaeng* date from the period of the Three Kingdoms (roughly 57 BC–AD 669), and rather than having first been associated with prostitution as in Japan, the *kisaeng* were young upper-class girls trained in singing, dancing and pleasuring men, and attached to the royal court for the pleasure of the king, senior ministers and important visitors.

At first called *yorak* (yoh-rahk), or entertainers, the number of these young women increased over the generations, and because they intermingled with men on the highest level in the country, they were often primary actors in illicit romances and scandals.

In the late 15th and early 16th century, the newly crowned king of the Choson dynasty increased the number of *kisaeng* attached to the court from 100 to 10,000 and referred to his chief *kisaeng* recruiter as his "red skirt envoy."

The royal recruiters scoured the country, looking for the prettiest girls—and once selected, they were the only females in the country who were permitted to become educated. Their training included reading, writing, composing poetry, playing musical instruments, singing and dancing. They were also instructed in a variety of topics designed to make them interesting conversationalists for men—something Korean wives did not do with their husbands.

Following this extraordinary move by the Choson king, recruiting, training, feeding, dressing and managing the *kisaeng* became a major commercial enterprise with hundreds of support personnel. They were the only women in Korea who could wear makeup and gorgeous clothing, and did not have to avert their eyes from passing males. They could also smile and talk as much as they pleased—something that was denied to other women.

Another rule established by the Choson king was that all *kisaeng* had to retire at the age of 30—so they could be replaced by young girls who had been recruited when they were eight or nine years old, and trained until they were 15 and became full-fledged *kisaeng*.

Although *kisaeng* were officially prohibited from marrying, the majority became mistresses and some became second wives. Many became nationally famous for their beauty and artistic accomplishments, and some became wealthy as a result of gifts from rich patrons.

There were several categories and ranks of *kisaeng* during the last centuries of the Choson era, including one category that was trained as doctors to administer to women, since male doctors were not permitted to touch female patients in any way at any time.

During the last century of the Choson dynasty (it ended in 1910), the thousands of *kisaeng* attached to the royal court were made available to all upper-class men who could afford their fees. The older sons and fathers in many families bankrupted themselves in their pursuit of the pleasure girls.

The *kisaeng* formed a union between 1897 and 1906, separated from the royal court in 1910, and came under the control of private managers.

Today, every city of any size has its *kisaeng* houses, and while they include some of the most beautiful women in the world, their skills are generally limited to dancing, singing, talking and making men feel good. Some of the *kisaeng* (and nightclub hostesses) are, in fact, so gorgeous that Western patrons are likely to drool at the sight of them.

Taking guests to *kisaeng* houses is an integral part of the Korean way of establishing and sustaining business relationships. Most foreign businesspeople who go to Korea and have Korean contacts are taken to *kisaeng* houses for dinner and entertainment.

The Job Rotation System

Larger Korean corporations typically rotate their younger white-collar employees among departments and branches in the early spring as part of their on-the-job training. This system is referred to as *insa idong* (een-sah ee-dong) or "job rotation."

The purpose of this system is, of course, to familiarize new managerial and executive candidates with all of the key departments and divisions of the company, and to ensure that they become acquainted with others to facilitate communication in the years ahead.

There are obviously many benefits to the *insa idong* system, but it has a downside as well, not only for the company itself, but also for foreign businesspeople who deal with the company. Because key sections in the company have a regular stream of new people who are inexperienced, the overall productivity of the sections is lower than what it would be if staffed only by veterans.

Since the purpose of rotating young employees into new jobs is to give them experience, they are assigned tasks they have never done before and must go through a learning curve. One of the tasks that is typically assigned to newcomers in sections and departments is interfacing with foreign visitors and customers.

It therefore often happens that managing the product or service of a foreign company is left in the hands of young people with limited experience. It takes anywhere from one or two years to three or four years, for a foreign company to develop a good, efficient and productive relationship with a Korean agent or joint-venture partner—a process that can be adversely affected by having to deal with a new contact every year or so. About the only practical way to counter what can be a serious handicap caused by the *insa idong* system is to keep the section or department chiefs and their deputies in the communications loop so they will be informed of what is, or is not, going on.

However, if foreign companies can hang in and succeed in Korea despite the job rotating system, it can gradually become a significant plus in their overall relationships and success—because they will end up knowing managers in many parts of the Korean company.

Company Mottos and Creeds

Any understanding and appreciation of Korean etiquette and ethics in business must include the values and expectations incorporated in the word *sahun* (sah-hoon), which translates as "company instructions," but in reality is more of a statement or motto that encapsulates a company's corporate philosophy and goals.

Both the philosophy and goals of the typical Korean company, as expressed in its *sahun*, are invariably based on the highest ethical and moral standards, on insuring the survival and growth of the company, and making a contribution to society and the nation.

Thus, *sahun* are designed to have the practical, nationalistic and spiritual content that the Korean psyche demands. Among the elements that are typically found in company mottos are expressions that come under the term *chango* (chahng-goh), which refers to creativity and entrepreneurial spirit.

In addition to *sahun*, Korean companies also have *jimmu kyuchik* (jeem-muu k'yuu-cheek), or company rules, and a reading of the rules of a particular company reveals a great deal about the etiquette and ethics that are aimed at shaping and controlling the conduct of employees in that company.

Foreign companies setting up operations in Korea are well advised to come up with *sahun* of their own that fit the sentiments and aspirations of their employees, along with company rules that spell out, precisely, the terms of employment down to the last dot.

Dealing With Office Stress

Pulda (puhl-dah) is the Korean term for office stress—that is, the stress that builds up in Korean companies because of having to conform to precise rules of etiquette and to work at an inhumanly fast pace in a highly competitive atmosphere.

While foreign managers in Korea seldom if ever, attempt to use full-fledged Korean management techniques, there is invariably some degree of *pulda* buildup in any group of Koreans because of the requirements of their etiquette and because they set such high standards for themselves.

Both Korean and foreign companies deal with the *pulda* factor by organizing and sponsoring periodic events that are designed to relieve stress. These include sporting events, and eating and drinking parties at which inferiors and superiors can behave more or less as equals, temporarily dispensing with the strict protocol that controls their behavior at other times.

These *pulda*-relieving events sometimes include humorous skits in which the roles of inferiors and superiors are switched, with lower ranking employees getting to order their bosses around—a cultural tradition that is ancient in Korea.

In fact, during Korea's long feudal age, the only way common people could criticize superiors, the social system and the government as a whole, was in humorous plays that were presented as entertainment.

Now that the feudal system is no longer the law of the land and the calm that was long associated with Korea is no longer enforced with a heavy hand, most urban Koreans live in the fast lane, with all of the tension that one can experience driving down a crowded freeway at well above the speed limit.

The pace of business in Korea is such that many Western resident and visiting businesspeople can't wait to get back to New York or some other such place where life is much slower.

Advice for Foreign Managers

Harmonious labor-management relations in Korea require a much larger personal commitment of time and resources than is typical in the average Western company. International business consultant Song-Hyon Jang, president of S. H. Jang and Associates Inc., lists some of the keys to achieving the necessary harmony—multilevel communications, a competitive compensation package, interpersonal company activities, scrupulously fair treatment and a documented work policy.

"It is particularly important for expatriate managers to open natural but discreet communications channels with their Korean staff, on different levels in all departments," notes Jang. "A deliberate avoidance of bureaucratic protocol will make the head office more accessible to the employees, allowing lines of communication to develop. As long as there is a conscious effort to remove all obstacles and restrictions to a free flow of communication between labor and management, disputes can be prevented or defused. However, in communication with labor, management has to preserve a benevolent but firm and consistent position. Koreans have learned how to respect authority," he adds.

Avoiding Cultural Backlash

Although the Western concept of democracy has taken firm root in Korea, Western individualism is not as deeply or as wholeheartedly accepted because it goes against the cultural conditioning that has long been the foundation of Korean society.

Koreans appreciate the concept of *tongnip* (tohn-neep), or personal "independence," in principle, and they apply it to their lives in areas that do not directly impact on others. But Korean society as a whole still functions on the ancient Confucian concept of groupism. Individualistic behavior within a group situation generally creates friction and ill will.

Many Koreans, particularly those who are more traditional, tend to look upon Western-style individualism and independence as selfishness since it gives precedence to the individual, often at the expense of others around them.

It pays for the foreign businessperson in Korea and those doing business with Korea, to be sensitive to any possible backlash resulting from demonstrating and expecting or demanding, individualistic behavior from their Korean contacts.

The Role of "Go-Betweens"

Unlike the US and other Western countries, the tradition in Korea was for disputes to be handled by *chungjaein* (chuung-jay-een), or private mediators, rather to use a legal system of lawyers, judges and courts.

In feudal Korea (prior to 1910), the legal system consisted of a relatively small number of edicts published by the various Courts over hundreds of years—most of which were based on Confucian principles—and government officials who had acted as judge and jury on their own.

The Confucian oriented Court did not believe in establishing comprehensive laws to govern the populace, preferring instead give authorities at various levels leeway to make their own rulings and to interpret existing laws according to the circumstances.

Because decisions made by existing authorities were therefore arbitrary and generally not based on the Western concept of justice or fairness, people with disputes avoided going to the authorities with their problems, preferring instead to use *chungjaein*.

Since the downfall of the Choson dynasty in 1910, and especially since the implementation of a democratic form of government from around 1960, Korea has established a legal system that is patterned more or less, after the Western system.

Still today, however, there are fundamental differences in Korea's approach to the law and dispute settlement. Until the 1990s, lawyers did not "work for" their clients. They worked for the courts, and their primary purpose was to represent the government and the government's interpretation of laws.

This situation has improved considerably and there are now lawyers who represent clients in the Western sense. But generally speaking, Koreans still prefer to use *chungjaein* to settle disputes because it goes against their cultural grain to get involved with government authorities on any level and in any way.

Western businesspeople are well advised to first take the mediator approach to settling any problems they have in Korea—going to the courts only as a last resort, and keeping in mind that the level of "justice" in Korea continues to vary with the topic, the parties in a dispute, and the region of the country where the situation occurs.

Just as foreign companies operating in Korea should have a good Korean consultant on staff, it also makes good sense to have access to people who have a good track record as professional mediators.

The Need for Patience

When the foreigner first arrives in Korea, whether to engage in business or diplomacy, one of the many things he or she is told is that the most important attribute they must have is *chamulsong* (chah-muhl-song), or patience—that without almost infinite patience, their path will be hard and much less likely to lead them to success.

While Korean philosophers looked upon *chamulsong* as being one of the Koreans' most admirable traits, they did not bother to consider that Koreans had to be patient because they had absolutely no viable choice.

Historically, any attempt to speed things beyond what was morally and culturally acceptable was so un-Korean that it could be life threatening. Such changes were not only seen as anti-Confucian, they were also politically forbidden because the reigning powers liked things the way they were.

Patience is still a very important element in doing business in Korea because of both continuing cultural restraints on taking fast actions before a solid consensus is reached, and the fact that the government agencies involved in guiding and controlling business activities tend to be bureaucratic.

Further, government bureaucrats in Korea do not necessarily follow the letter of the law in approving things. There is typically a personal and an emotional element in their behavior that can add days, weeks or months to their actions, and often require that considerable outside pressure and/or some other step be taken by the petitioner before a matter is settled.

On an individual basis, Koreans can be as impatient and as outspoken as anyone else. But when it involves a company or a government agency, they generally cannot act on their own and must be very circumspect in dealing with others so as not to make things worse.

Naturally, the larger the number of people who are involved or may be involved in any situation, the longer it generally takes to achieve a consensus and get action. Overt efforts to speed things up in a non-Korean way are more likely to slow them down.

Formula for Keeping Best Workers

Consultant S.H. Jang says that for the foreign company in Korea to achieve sustained growth and success, it is imperative for it to have a competitive compensation scheme, otherwise the company will continuously lose its best workers to other firms with better pay packages.

When companies are too small to be competitive in direct compensation, or have budgetary constraints for any reason, Jang recommends such benefits as stock offers, pension plans, unemployment insurance and health care plans.

Developing Team Spirit

One of the most effective ways to build team spirit and a family-like atmosphere in the foreign company in Korea is to sponsor such activities as picnics, sports activities, a company newsletter or newspaper and recreational clubs.

Perhaps the most important aspect of managing a Korean work force is to be scrupulously fair to all employees and avoid favoring any particular employee for any reason. "It is sometimes necessary to go beyond the stipulations of labor law," says consultant Jang, "especially where family members of top executives are involved in the organization."

Jang adds: "Without compromising standards, the manager's handling of mistakes made by staff members requires a great deal of diplomacy and understanding to prevent them from losing face. To avoid office tension and belligerence, fair just treatment by the manager is crucial. Proper treatment will tend to weld the loyalty of office personnel to the manager and raise the degree of efficiency and quality of their work." Jang further notes that it is essential for foreign employers to put their employment regulations, office procedures and work rules in writing and have them signed by all new incoming employees.

"Once a complaint is filed by an employee against company executives, labor authorities tend to support the employee, so a signed agreement can save a lot of trouble," Jang added.

The Use of Collective Punishment

One of the primary foundations of traditional Confucian societies (and Korea was long been described as the most Confucian of all Asian nations, including China) was collective responsibility and *chebol* (chehbohl), or collective punishment.

In early Korea, *chebol* was practiced with religious zeal as one of the measures to maintain absolute stability. Whole families and whole villages were held responsible for the behavior of each member—an inhuman system that turned people into virtual robots obsessed with following prescribed rules and customs.

Chebol is not a part of modern-day Korea's legal system, but it remains in the psyche of older Koreans, resulting in them being especially watchful and concerned about the behavior of family members.

Koreans are especially sensitive about being subjected to collective punishment of any kind, in any way, particularly by foreign countries and foreign companies. Foreign business managers in Korea should therefore be especially careful to individualize any sanctions they might impose on employees.

Veterans' Law

Because of its system of mandatory military service for all males, the ROK has a Veterans' Administration Law that requires all firms in Korea with 20 or more employees to hire veterans, their spouses and their children, in proportion to the overall number of employees. All foreign companies setting up operations in Korea are subject to this law and must take it into consideration in their hiring practices.

When employers are unable to find their minimum quota of veterans and their family members, the government provides them.

Foreign Workers

Korean companies have few racial or cultural qualms about employing Western workers in their domestic offices and factories. Major employers of foreign talent include the country's top conglomerates such as Hyundai, Samsung and LG. Among the hundreds of such employees are engineers, scholars, consultants and attorneys.

Emphasis on Company Training

Larger Korean companies have rigorous procedures for selecting new employees, with each company striving to get the best and brightest of the annual crop of university graduates. The process begins with stiff screening examinations in which the competition may be as high as 100 to one. Once accepted into a company, an equally rigorous training program lasting from two to five months, and incorporating both "brain-washing" and "survival techniques," begins. The purpose of the training programs goes beyond just giving the new employee the necessary knowledge and skills to make a contribution to the company's efforts. They are aimed at molding the newcomers to fit the company's organizational pattern and culture.

The training tends to emphasize attitude instead of professional skills—the idea being that dedication, loyalty and team spirit take precedence over job skill. It also includes intensive courses in foreign languages, particularly English, with the trainees sometimes being sent to university-level language institutes. The companies thus make a long-term investment in their most promising managerial candidates.

Samsung Co. Ltd., founded in 1938 and generally listed as the oldest company in Korea's business history, is famous—or notorious, depending on the source—for its managerial system and its personnel training program, which has been described as "incredibly inhuman." Because of its emphasis on tough training for its employees, the company is frequently referred to as the "Samsung Academy," and is regarded as a training center for Korean businesspeople.

Samsung's founder, Byung-Chull Lee, carried "report cards" on every executive in the company, and used the cards at the beginning of each new year to decide who was to be promoted or demoted.

Arbitration Taboos

As is typical in Confucian oriented societies, Koreans abhor the idea of outsiders becoming involved in their business affairs, which they regard as personal.

Until recent times, Western-style arbitration was not regarded as a logical or viable choice. When Koreans were forced to accept arbitration, the decisions were invariably Korean-style compromises—the kind of solution they preferred to find on their own.

Times have changed. There is now a Korean Arbitration Board (KAB) that is very active, and is generally held in high regard by the foreign business community. English language translations are provided, and in some cases, the proceedings are conducted in English. But arbitration under the KAB may be lengthy and expensive.

Amcham continues to advise foreign companies to attempt to get the use of American or ICC arbitration rules in Geneva written into any joint-venture agreement, while noting, however, that the Korean side may strongly oppose the move. If opposition does occur, the only recourse may be patience and persistence.

The moral, of course, is to avoid the official arbitration process in Korea. Koreans abhor the idea of *chungjae*, or "arbitration by outsiders," and go to extreme lengths to avoid it. They regard such a move by company executives as a public admission of their incompetency and general unfitness to direct a company's affairs.

However, private "mediation" between the parties involved in a dispute, which is the same word in Korean, is the accepted method of resolving disputes. The experienced mediator (*chungjae-in*) is therefore an important person in Korean society. *Chungjae-in* also means "middleman" and "intermediary."

The Importance of the Apology

In Confucian oriented societies, the apology has traditionally played a similar role to that of confessions in the Catholic religion where you confess your sins, God forgives you, and you have a clean slate.

The traditional etiquette in Korea—which covered all personal as well as official relationships—was so detailed, so strict and so limiting that mistakes and general failures to live up to all of the requirements were so common that apologizing, often even before an event took place, became an institutionalized and virtually ritualized custom.

When individuals committed relatively minor infractions of the law or any law-like custom that resulted in the authorities becoming involved, a teary *sagwa* (sahg-wah), or apology, was often enough to get one off with no more than a reprimand. It the offense was serious, an apology mitigated the level of punishment. However, if one refused to apologize for the offense—guilty or not—the punishment was invariably much more harsh.

The *sagwa* continues to play an important role in Korean society, in personal as well as business and professional relationships. Some offenses require only a verbal apology. Others require a *simal so* (she-mahl soh) or "letter of apology."

Foreigners in Korea, businesspeople as well as others, should be aware of the importance of the apology in the etiquette and ethics of Koreans, and make appropriate use of it.

Because of the strict system of etiquette, Koreans find that frequent apologies on all kinds of occasions, including what may appear to be trifling concerns to outsiders, are the better part of valor.

The Korean Adaptation of English

Korea, like Japan, has adopted thousands of English words and made them a key part of the Korean vocabulary. Unlike the Japanese, however, Koreans do not feel compelled to Koreanize everything that comes into the country.

One good example of this is their different treatment of foreign words that are adopted into their languages. In Japan, many foreign words are Japanized and pronounced as if they were Japanese—with the result that it is often extremely difficult and sometimes, impossible for foreign students of Japanese to divine the meaning of the formerly English terms.

An example of one such term: *sabaiburu* (sah-by-buu-ruu), which is "survival" pronounced in Japanese. However, unless read or heard in very clear and specific context, *sabaiburu* is meaningless to the native English speaker.

Rather than go this same route as the Japanese, the Korean Ministry of Education (in 1985) adopted a system of writing foreign words in the Korean alphabet that maintains as far as possible, the original pronunciation. This farsighted move has made a significant contribution to the ability of Koreans and English-speaking people to communicate with one another.

Do's and Don'ts

Every foreign businessperson who has spent any significant length of time in Korea has his own list of Dos and Don'ts for doing business in the ROK. Virtually all of these lists begin with: establish a network of strong personal friendships inside and outside of the government, and nurture them carefully and continuously.

Almost all actions one takes, personal and business, are fundamentally influenced by one's network of friends. The government plays such an important role in business in Korea that it is essential to identify the appropriate ministries, agencies, offices and officials as early as possible in order to immediately begin the process of developing and massaging that network.

Your commitment to Korea should be long-term, and the man who comes in and sets up the operation, whatever it is, should be prepared to remain in Korea for several years—a minimum of three, and this is cutting it very thin. When transfers are made, it is vital that the replacement be brought in early—like a year or more—to give him time to take over the network of friends and contacts that have been built up.

And again, this is not something that can be handled "American-style," just by taking the newcomer around, introducing him and then leaving him on his own. The depth and quality of personal relationships necessary to function effectively in Korea comes only with time. Patience, good emotional control, a sense of humor and a long-term perspective are essential for doing well in Korea.

Despite appearances, it is generally unwise to leave important decisions—or in many cases, routine decisions—to the Korean side, even when you are dealing with a very internationalized individual with extensive experience, unless you are willing to accept the consequences of decisions reflecting a strong Korean flavor. Along the same line, the foreign businessperson in Korea cannot leave marketing arrangements up to personal connections although personal relationships may play a key role in setting up a marketing program.

Other hard-knocks wisdom suggested by veteran businesspeople on the scene: don't leave government approval up to a Korean partner;

don't locate a joint-venture firm in the same building as your Korean partner; and make sure you control (with experienced advice) all hiring and placement.

Regulation by Competitors

As extraordinary as it might seem, there are several industries in which Korean companies in effect regulate the activities of their foreign competitors. These industries include advertising, banking, insurance, transportation companies, trading companies, engineering companies and construction companies.

Generally, this regulation is effected through industry associations that foreign firms cannot join, or if they can join they are limited to the type of membership that has no power or influence. In the case of the airline industry, however, Korean Air directly regulates the activities of foreign airlines serving Korea.

One of the techniques traditionally used by industry associations to control the behavior of foreign competitors was to enact non-tariff barriers that made it difficult or impossible for the foreign firms to do business—a situation that the Korean government has been working to resolve, with some success.

The Prime Contact for Newcomers

The most important contact for any foreign company proposing to do business in or with Korea is the American Chamber of Commerce (AmCham) in Seoul. The Chamber is a strong, vocal advocate on behalf of foreign business, and has accumulated a substantial amount of information and insight on the laws, regulations and subtleties of doing business in the country.

Among the 32 Chamber-member committees that contribute to these insights are banking, financial services, intellectual property, joint ventures, labor, living and civil affairs, ROK government liaison, taxation and the US Government, trade expansion and transportation.

The Chamber sponsors briefing meetings for individual companies on a monthly basis, providing newcomers with the insights and guidance of a number of old-timers who have learned the ropes (often the hard way) in years of experience in Korea.

Depending on the kind of business you want to do in or with Korea, the Amcham can direct you to other sources of information and help, from the Commercial Section of the US Embassy and branches of foreign banks to appropriate Korean government agencies and offices. Direct contacts to:

American Chamber of Commerce in Korea
#4501 Trade Tower, 159-1, Samsung-Dong, Kangnam-Gu
Seoul, Korea 135-729
Tel (82-2) 564-2040; fax (82-2) 564-2050
www.amchamkorea.org; info@amchamkorea.org

The Good Side

Despite the many cultural and political handicaps involved in doing business in Korea, there are even more compensations that make the effort worthwhile for a growing number of foreign businesspeople. On a personal level, Koreans are a sincere, warm and friendly people who have often been described as "the Irish of the Orient." They make deep commitments of friendship and loyalty that are permanent if they are treated fairly and with respect. By the same token, if they are mistreated, they make formidable enemies.

It is the personal quality of life and thought in Korea that attracts so many Westerners to persevere in the face of professional and political obstacles. They have come to love and admire Koreans and have become greatly attached to many aspects of the culture.

In a strictly business context, the ROK represents a large, growing market with a highly disciplined work force, few labor problems, a high standard of education, an overwhelming ambition to better itself economically and socially, and rapidly rising expectations.

A significant percentage of Korea's top managers were educated in the US. They not only speak English well, they are especially friendly toward the US. These foreign-educated Koreans in particular, are imbued with an extraordinary "can do" spirit that is exciting and catching, and augurs well for Korea.

Another special advantage that foreigners have in Korea is that Koreans feel more at ease with foreigners. Unlike the average Japanese, they do not find associating with or dealing with foreigners such an emotional burden, and are therefore able to deal more effectively with non-Koreans. Japanese businesspeople continuously comment on how tiring and nerve-racking it is for them to be in close contact with Westerners, even when they (the Japanese) speak English fairly well. Koreans, on the other hand, seem to thrive on associating with foreigners and are much more aggressive in their relationships.

Koreans are very conscious of their long history and the great arts and crafts achievements of their civilization. This consciousness has been translated into official government policy, which mandates that the cultural heritage of the country be protected and incorporated in the national infrastructure. This concern for and use of art adds a special ambience to life in Korea that is growing more common and significant with each passing year. It adds to the attraction of living and working in Korea, and is a definite plus for the foreign community.

CHAPTER FOUR

Vocabulary of the Korean Way

Achom (ah-choam)—In Korea, it is very important to maintain a positive, friendly demeanor and avoid hurting anyone's feelings. Part of this process consists of the generous use of compliments and flattery, or *achom*. Foreigners not familiar with the social custom are likely to confuse such flattery and compliments with extraordinary politeness, and a friendly, easygoing and cooperative attitude. While the latter may be true on an individual basis, the practice of *achom* has a far more serious purpose. See *kibun*.

Amukuto anida (ah-muu-kuu-toe ah-nee-dah)—A common response when someone in Korea is given a hard task. It means "It's nothing. I can do it easily," and is indicative of the "can do" spirit of Koreans.

Apatu (ah-pah-tuu)—The size and location of an *apatu* (apartment) is of special importance in Korea because it is associated with social class, which in turn is an important factor in the type of work one is able to obtain and where one works. Foreign managers in Korea should be aware of the class factor and take it into account in their dealings and relationships with Korean employees.

Chakupjachok (chah-kuup-jah-choke)—The Self-Sufficiency Syndrome. Given Korea's historical circumstance—divided by exclusive clans and by regional kingdoms that were usually on the outs with each other, and being surrounded by countries that were hostile and invaded and occupied the whole peninsula several times—it was natural for Koreans on all levels, from individual families, to attempt to be as self-sufficient as possible.

This self-sufficiency syndrome was the driving force behind the attempts of post-World War II companies in Korea to grow into huge combines that did everything—from controlling the raw materials they needed, to the retailing process. (It also became the mantra of North Korea's isolated Communist leaders.)

Foreign companies dealing with Korea invariably run into the self-sufficiency concept, which remains a primary factor in the policies and practices of the government because the country's leaders are determined that Korea will never again come under the political or economic hegemony of any foreign power.

That said, both government and business leaders now understand that Korea must continue the globalization process of the economy in order to continue to fulfill the potential of the people, and contribute to the peace and prosperity of the world.

But they still have a long way to go, and both businesspeople and diplomats involved with Korea should be prepared to deal with this powerful syndrome.

Bokshin (boak-sheen)—*Bokshin* refers to an aide or assistant who is so trusted by the boss that he is allowed to act on his behalf. The literal meaning of the term is, roughly, "man in his belly."

Bural an chok (buu-rahl ahn choak)—A man who builds up a business enterprise with hard work but little capital is said to have done it *bural an chok*, or "only with balls."

Byul jang (buul jahng)—Literally a remote house, this is the Korean word for a recreational villa, usually on the coast or in the mountains. Many of the *byul jang* in Korea are maintained by large companies for their employees.

Chaebol (chay-bowl)—This is the term used in reference to Korea's huge business-industrial complexes such as Hyundai, Samsung, LG (formerly Lucky and Goldstar) and the SK Group. It is the Korean equivalent of the well-known Japanese term *zaibatsu*.

Chagayong unjonsa (chah-gah-yong uun-joan-sah)— Just as in other countries, personal chauffeurs (*chagayong unjonsa*) are a highly prized status symbol in Korea. They are especially practical for businesspeople who work in the downtown areas of Seoul and other major Korean cities because of the scarcity of parking places.

Chehan (chay-hahn)—This is the word for restriction, which is often used in Korea, particularly in relation to imports and exports.

Chibaein (chee-by-een)—Koreans take such titles as *chibaein* (manager) very seriously, and it is common to address them by their titles instead of by their names, particularly since so many people have the same family name (in a company with 100 employees, as many as ten or more may be named Lee, another ten or so may be named Pak, and there may be ten or more Kims, etc.).

Chido (chee-doe)—This is the Korean equivalent of the Japanese term *shido*, which is used in connection with government "guidance" of industry. It is somewhat less commonly used in Korea because there is very little effort to disguise or deny that the government's role is more in the nature of control than guidance.

Chim shin uro (cheem sheen uu-roe)—The Korean term for "pure heart," *chim shin uro* is used in reference to a person of impeccable integrity and sincerity, one who can be depended upon to do what is right. It is a quality Korean employers pay special attention to in their hiring practices.

Chinchok (cheen-choke)—Korea's strong family orientation extends well beyond the nuclear family to include relatives (*chinchok*) two, three and four times removed. This sometimes complicates their relationships with Westerners. The foreigner who marries a Korean is often surprised at the size of the "family" he or she has acquired (and is obligated to in many ways).

Chip an (cheep ahn)—The Korean equivalent of the Japanese *uchi*, used in the sense of "my house," "my home," "my company." *Chip an* literally means "inside the house" and is used in the same way as the Japanese word. The usage indicates the close relationship Koreans develop with their place of employment, putting it on the level of their home.

Chisongnyok (chee-song-nyoke)—This is the term used by Koreans in reference to their incredible capacity to endure physical and mental stress. It is seen as one of their major national strengths.

Chohoe (choe-hay)—The morning meeting or "morning ceremony" (*chohoe*) has been adopted by most major Korean companies, and the practice is growing. The *chohoe* held by some companies is very ceremonial—in some, the national anthem is played.

Chonmae (chone-my)—The Korean government operates a number of monopolies (*chonmae*) as a method of earning income. The monopolized products include ginseng and tobacco.

Chongchi (chong-chee)—Politics (*chongchi*) plays a role in almost every foreign business deal consummated in Korea, so this is a useful word to know. Another important word is *chongbu*, meaning government.

Chong ddae (chong-dday)—Literally "the barrel of a gun," this is the Korean version of "hired gun," or someone who does an unpleasant job for the boss.

Chongui (chong-we)—The Korean concept of justice (*chongui*) is based more on what is good for society and the country than on what is best for the individual. Because of this philosophical difference, foreigners who become involved in court cases in Korea are often disappointed with the outcome.

Chongyong (chone-gyong)—Because of the vertical structure of their society and the importance of maintaining and protecting one's social status, Koreans are very sensitive about paying and being paid proper respect (*chongyong*). Foreigners living and working in Korea must learn something about this etiquette and make use of it in order to function effectively.

Chonmae tuko (chone-my tuu-kah)—In Korea, foreign patents (*chonmae tuko*) must be registered in both Korean and the language of the originating country.

Chonmun-ga (chone-muun-gah)—While the idea of paying a consulting fee or a royalty to someone for their advice or the use of their intellectual achievements is basically foreign to Koreans, they still recognize the value of *chonmun-ga*, or experts, and make use of a growing number of foreign consultants, engineers and scientists.

Chuchon (chuu-chone)—A *chuchon*, or recommendation, is very important in making new contacts in Korea. The recommendation may be written or verbal. The best is verbal and in person.

Chukcheil (chuke-chay-eel)—Folk festivals (*chukcheil*), many of them dating before recorded history and shamanistic in origin, continue to play a vital role in the lives of most Koreans. They are especially important events in rural areas.

Chulhyong sawon (chule-hyong sah-woan)—This is a worker or employee on loan to an affiliated or subsidiary firm. It generally carries the connotation that it is a temporary situation, but the transfer may also be permanent. Valued employees are often sent out to help rescue smaller affiliated companies that have gotten into trouble. It is also a common practice when one company acquires another firm, either to control it or to assist its management.

Chusik hoesa (chuu-sheek hoe-eh-sah)—A stock company. This is the most common type of company organization in Korea.

Daedulpo (day-duul-poe)—Literally "stone and pillar." Figuratively, the person in an office, agency or company who is primarily responsible for keeping it going and for its success. "Stone" refers to a foundation stone, and "pillar" to what holds a building up. The "backbone" of the company.

Daepochip (day-poe-cheep)—This is the Korean equivalent of the Japanese word *akachin* (ah-kah-cheen) or red lantern, symbolic of drinking and drinking establishments. However, the literal meaning of *daepochip* is something like "house of artillery" or a place where big guns are kept. The inference is that when people drink they often shoot off their mouths. The more they drink, the bigger become the "shots" they fire. Red lanterns are not hung in front of Korean drinking places, as they are in Japan.

Dollah box (dollar box)—A company's most profitable product, line or department is frequently referred to as its dollar box. A company's source of financing may also be called its dollar box.

Dong chang saeng (dong chahng sang)—A Korean businessperson's biggest asset is his *dong chang saeng*, or "network," made up of classmates, alumni brothers, friends made in the military, relatives, relations by marriage and other close friends he has made along the way. The foreign businessperson in Korea must take the same approach to develop his own network.

Danyom hada (dahn-yoam hah-dah)—This is the Korean equivalent of throwing in the towel or giving up or dropping something, such as negotiations that are not going anywhere or a product that is losing money. The literal translation is something like "cutting one's mind."

Dulinda (duu-leen-dah)—This is a commonly used greeting among businesspeople in Korea when they make courtesy calls on customers or contacts. It means, more or less, "Are you at peace?" in reference to the fact that Korea has experienced so much warfare in its history. The present-day meaning is something like, "Are things going well?"

Gara mungeida (gah-rah muun-gay-dah)—Literally "to crush with one's rear end," this is the equivalent of killing a proposal or application by sitting on it, something that government bureaucrats in Korea and elsewhere are often accused of.

Haengjong (hang-joang)—While generally following Confucian principles, the *haengjong*, or administration, in Korean companies is often significantly affected by the personal style of the president or chairperson, and when several members of the same family are involved in top management.

Hachong (hah-chong)—All of Korea's large, well-known companies have a network of *hachong* (subcontract firms) beneath them. Just as in Japan and other countries, the subcontract firms are used as cushions to shield the major companies from fluctuations in demand, prices and exchange rates.

Hakuksang (hah-kuuk-sahng)—In Korea's tightly structured vertical society, *hakuksang*, or "going over a superior's head," is a very serious matter. Management ranks in larger companies are as clearly defined and as guarded as those in the military.

Hangugo (hahn-guu-go)—The Korean language.

Hanguk (hahn-gook)—This is the Korean word for Korea. It means "Great Country." *Hangug-in* (hahn-goog-een) means Korean person.

Hanguk umshik (hahn-gook uum-sheek) or **hanshik** (hahn-sheek)—This is the term for Korean food, which the visitor will find very useful. If you don't want to eat Korean food every day, it is also advisable to learn how to say *yang shik* (foreign food).

Hangul (hahn-guul)—The Korean system of writing—the special phonetic characters used to write the language—was developed by a team of scholars in the early 1400s at the request of King Sejong. It is the only writing system known to have been deliberately designed by a group of experts over a short period of time. The symbols can be learned in a day or so, as opposed to the many months or years required to learn the ideograms used in Japan and China (and to a lesser and decreasing degree in Korea).

Hanjan hapshida (hahnjahn hop-she-dah)—A commonly heard term in Korea's business world, this is the equivalent of "let's have a drink." It is rare, however, for the guest to get by with having only one drink. Korean businesspeople tend to put as much enthusiasm and energy into drinking as they do working.

Han jan man (hahn jahn mahn)—*Han jan man,* or "only one glass," is the common Korean invitation used to invite someone out for a drink and a talk, usually after business hours. "Only one glass" should not be taken literally.

Hapcha Hoesa (hop-chah hoe-eh-sah)—A limited partnership company.

Hapmyng Hoesa (Hop-ming hoe-eh-sah)—A partnership company, a form of company organization that is rare in Korea.

Hoegyesa (Hoag-yay-sah)—The *hoegyesa,* or accountant, in a Korean firm is an important individual. It is very helpful for the foreign businessperson to establish a strong personal relationship with the *hoegyesa.*

Huisaeng ta (hwee-sang tah)—Literally a "sacrifice batter," this is a person sent in to learn as much as possible before serious negotiations start, or used some other way as a front man who plays an early limited role to gain a fast advantage.

Hukmak (huke-mahk)—It is common in Korea for an individual behind the scenes (*hukmak*) to be the one who really exercises power. *Hukmak* means "black curtain." Another term is *makhu shil yokja* (mahk-huu sheel yoakjah), which means "strong man behind a curtain."

Hwandae (hwahn-die)—This is the word for Korea's famous hospitality, which can be overwhelming, but pays off in the goodwill and cooperation that it generates.

Hwanyong hoe (whan-yong hay)—Koreans are noted for their elaborate *hwanyong hoe*, or welcoming receptions, which are part of their custom of conspicuous hospitality. They are customary when welcoming new employees into a company and when formally greeting newly arrived guests, especially from abroad.

Hyongshikchogin (h'yong-sheek-choe-gheen)—Korean businesspeople and government officials tend to be *hyongshikchogin* (formal) in their behavior, especially toward foreign guests.

Hyopoe (hyahp-po-eh)—Associations (*hyopoe*) are a vital aspect of business as well as personal affairs in Korea. Generally speaking, many of the associations having to do with business constitute obstacles to foreign companies dealing with Korea, since they are exclusive and are designed to give the Korean members an advantage over foreign companies.

Ilbonsaram (eel-bone-sah-rahm)—This word means Japanese (person), and is something Koreans do not like to be mistaken for. Generally speaking, Korean men are physically larger and more muscular than Japanese men, and the women are taller and have larger busts and wider hips than their Japanese counterparts.

Ilbulrae (eel-buul-ray)—"Working like an insect" is the Korean equivalent of a workaholic. The term is used often, generally in a positive, complimentary way. As one man said, "In Korea, the person who works like a bee is respected."

Inhwa (inn-whah)—A key principle of traditional Korean society, *inhwa* means harmony, in this case, based on Confucian concepts of hierarchical relationships between people, respect for elders, obedience to authority, coordinated group behavior and decisions by consensus.

In maek (inn make)—These are the personal connections that are so essential to both private and business life in Korea. Instead of going from the objective to the subjective, as is common in the West, virtually all relations in Korea start with the subjective or personal side. The importance of these personal connections is suggested by the term *in maek*, which means something like "human pulse."

Ipto ssagi (eep-toe sah-ghee)—This refers to the practice of hiring high school or university students before they graduate, in order to get the pick of the "crop." The word literally means "standing rice," and originally referred to brokers buying rice before it was harvested. It is also used in reference to buying stocks or merchandise before it is made or while it is still in the factory.

Jaebul (jay-buul)—Many companies in Korea belong to a specific *jaebul*, or group, and in various ways coordinate their operations with the leading firms heading up their groups. *Jaebul* is also used in reference to financial groups.

Jajunggu bakwi dolligi (jahjuung-guu bahk-we dole-leeghee)—A person who is being given the runaround by a company or government agency is said to *bejajunggu bakwi dolligi* or "pedaling a stationary bike." In other words, he isn't going anywhere.

Jal butak hamnida (jahl buu-tock hahm-nee-dah)—One of the most used phrases in the Korean language, this means something like "please do whatever you can for me." It is said to people when you want them to take care of something or do something, whether it is a favor or something they are obligated to do anyway. It is an institutionalized, stock phrase, and is the equivalent of Japan's *yoroshiku onegaishimasu*. It is used in both informal and formal situations, and is a way of humbling yourself so the other person won't regard your request as arrogant.

Jang ki (jahng kee)—Koreans take great pride in their ability to sing or perform some other kind of entertaining skill, which they are regularly called upon to do at parties. They generally practice these skills in private, a custom that is called *jang ki*, or "favorite technique."

Jimmu kyuchik (jeem-muu kyu-cheek)—Company rules, something every company in Korea should have, and should require all new employees to sign as one of the conditions of employment.

Joja sei (joejah-say-e)—It has historically been dangerous for individual Koreans to stand out in a crowd or to draw attention to themselves when things go wrong or when there is any kind of problem. Under these circumstances, it is common for them to *joja sei*, or "lay low." This can and often does cause additional problems in a company when keeping quiet compounds the situation.

Joong-in (joong-inn)—The *joong-in*, or upper-middle class, during Korea's long feudal period was made up mostly of professionals including doctors, lawyers, translators and middle-ranked military officers. The same groups are prominent in today's society, but are no longer hereditary or so clearly defined.

Junggi chaeyong (juung-ghee chay-yong)—This is "periodic hiring," and refers to the custom of Korean companies hiring high school and university graduates in batches in March, when the school year ends.

Jupan i anmaja (juu-pahn ee ahn-mahjah)—When Koreans feel that a price is too high, they are likely to say *jupan i anmaja* or that their "abacus is unbalanced."

Jwachon (jwah-choan)—Literally a "change to the left," this term refers to someone being demoted or transferred to a job with less prestige. It comes from the old custom of seating inferiors on the left.

Kanpan (kahn-pahn)—This is the Korean equivalent of the famous Japanese word *kanban*, which originally meant sign or bulletin board but now refers to the "just-in-time" delivery system made famous by Japanese manufacturers. Korean companies adapted the system to their own manufacturing process. The name originated from the practice initiated by a manager of Toyoda Loom Works of having a big overhead sign posted in the factory listing the parts that were to be delivered that day. Toyoda Loom Works was the forerunner of Toyota Motors Corporation.

Keiyul hoesa (kay-e-yuul hay-sah)—Korean companies are generally "aligned" with one of the major *chaebol* groups, and are known as *keiyul hoesa*, or affiliated companies. Which group a particular company belongs to can have a significant influence on its overall business, from its ability to raise capital to how effectively it can distribute and promote products in the Korean market. Foreign companies contemplating going into business with Korean firms should identify and familiarize themselves with their group afflliations.

Keo mul (kay-oh muul)—A man of exceptional power and influence is often referred to as a *keo mul*, or big shot.

Kibu (kee-buu)—Surprisingly, one of the "problems" of doing business in Korea is the pressure brought on companies to make frequent and sizeable *kibu* (donations) for causes that range from the very worthwhile to the very obscure and doubtful. It is often advisable to investigate groups soliciting donations before parting with your money. Even legitimate organizations tend to overdo it, however.

Kioe chae yong (kee-way chay yong)—This phrase means "hiring out-of-season," or the practice of hiring new employees at times other than following graduation, when most companies do their annual hiring.

Ko e kulmyun (koe ee kuul-me-uun), **Gui e kulmyun** (gwee ee kuul-me-uun)—These two terms mean "nose ring" and "earring," and are used in reference to a situation or thing (such as a contract) that can be interpreted in two or more ways, or a person who changes his attitude or position to suit the circumstances.

Kolpu (kole-puu)—This is Korean for golf, an activity that is seen by Korean businesspeople as an important part of their internationalizing.

Komun (koe-muun)—A Korean *komun* (consultant or advisor), especially one of high social standing with important government and industry contacts, can be invaluable to foreign companies in Korea or those wanting to do business with Korea. Retired government officials from key ministries as well as company executives from leading firms are also much in demand for their knowledge and network of contacts.

Kongja (kong-jah)—This is the Korean word for Confucius, perhaps the most important figure in Korean history. Familiarity with the primary teachings of Confucius is a great asset in understanding the attitudes and customs of Koreans.

Kongson (kong-soan)—Politeness (*kongson*), combined with Confucian-style respect, is one of the primary facets of the Korean social system. Koreans tend to be very formal in business and official relations. Generally speaking, businesspeople, government officials and other professionals in the company of foreigners relax completely only during nighttime drinking parties.

Korae (koe-ray)—Given the extraordinary compulsion Koreans have for bettering themselves, and the equally competitive nature of the economy, smaller independent businesspeople are constantly on the lookout for *korae*, or business deals. Their enthusiasm is so great it frequently bypasses their ability to perform. Newcomers should be aware of this factor and be sufficiently thorough in checking out potential business partners.

Kukche kyohon (kook-chay k'yoe-hoan)—International marriages (*kukche kyohon*), particularly between American men and Korean women, have been fairly commonplace since the early 1950s, when the US began stationing large numbers of troops and civilian workers there. Korean women have been renowned for ages for their beauty, strength, loyalty and other sterling qualities—to the extent that they were once regarded as one of the reasons why neighboring nations were motivated to conquer Korea.

Kukpiui (kook-pee-we)—With their family orientation, which extends to companies, Koreans do not think of such things as personal problems, financial affairs and the like as matters to be treated as confidential (*kukpiui*). This cultural characteristic often upsets foreigners who are not accustomed to such things being openly discussed, particularly matters concerning wages, bonuses and company business.

Kyesanso (kay-sahn-soe)—This is the kind of bill or check one gets in a restaurant, which frequently results in a tug-of-war or a flurry of arm wrestling with fellow Korean diners who will frequently try to take the bill by force and pay it. Many foreigners who are subjected to this physical assault give up the struggle fairly quickly, out of embarrassment, even when they know it is their place to pay.

Kyeyak (kay-yahk)—Because of the personal nature of the business system in Korea, a *kyeyak*, or contract, may be regarded as a personal arrangement between the individuals who signed it. This makes it extremely important for foreign companies to establish and maintain close personal relations with all levels of management in Korean firms they deal with.

Kyonbon (kyoan-bone)—Much to the surprise and dismay of foreign businesspeople, Korean customs often charge duties on product samples (*kyonbon*). Customs officials have a considerable amount of personal discretion in whether or not duties are charged, and at what rate.

Kyongjaeng (kyong-jang)—Competition (*kyongjaeng*) is a way of life in Korea. There is intense rivalry for the best education, the best job, the best of everything. Competition is on an individual, family, group, or company, as well as a national basis. It is one of the reasons for the remarkable economic advances made by Korea since the 1960s.

Kyosop (k'yoe-sop)—Koreans are skilled at negotiation (*kyosop*), in part because theirs is a very emotional culture with a highly refined verbal etiquette that makes it necessary for everyone to develop the ability to speak effectively, to manipulate the feelings of others and to be able to win by persuasion.

Kyoyuk (k'yoe-yuke)—Koreans are compulsive about getting an education (*kyoyuk*) because it has traditionally been one of the principal criteria for determining social class and advancement. For much of their long feudal history which actually did not end until 1945, only members of the hereditary upper class could aspire to a higher education and to positions of authority. Now that education is open to all and access to the official power structure is still decided on the basis of education, Korean parents go to extreme lengths to see that their children get the best possible education, with the greatest achievement being several years of postgraduate study in the US.

Kye (keh)—Cooperation and Mutual Help Pools. There is a deeply engrained personal and family aspect to doing business in Korea that is based on the pooling of funds and work to accomplish tasks and start new businesses. These mutual help groups get involved in such things as raising money to help celebrate auspicious birthdays of parents, to plan and stage weddings, to pay for funerals, to finance new businesses and to run "lottery pools" for wives.

All of these group efforts come under the word *kye* (keh), with means something like "agreement" or "bond."

Foreign businesspeople stationed in Korea can win considerable merit by making themselves aware of *kye* programs among their friends and employees, and making some kind of contribution to them.

Maeddugi hanchul (may-duu-ghee hahn-chuul)—This refers to the seasons when retail outlets are the busiest and make the most profits. The term literally means "grasshopper season," from the fact that during the short harvest season in Korea, grasshoppers eat with an intense frenzy, knowing that the food supply will disappear with the coming cold.

Mal i manta (mahl ee mahn-tah)—"Many words" or "one who talks too much," used in reference to a person who attempts to use logic over feelings, or cold reason over personal considerations. In Korea, people who try to use logic all the time and do a lot of talking are generally regarded with disdain, since this goes against the grain of a society based on human and personal feelings.

Mansei (mahn-say)—This is the Korean equivalent of the Japanese *banzai*, but its use is slightly different. In Korea it is most often used at sporting events when someone wins or does something spectacular. In business, it is customarily used to celebrate the signing of a contract or the accomplishment of an especially difficult task. It is a shout expressing pleasure and joy on an auspicious occasion. The closest English equivalent is "Hip! Hip! Hooray!"

Mitopop (meet-tah-pop)—This is Korean for the metric system, which is standard in Korea.

Mogaji (moe-gah-jee)—This is an old way of expressing the concept of dismissing or firing someone. It literally means to cut off one's head: *Mogaji taranada*, upon which the head flies away.

Mojo (moe-joe)—Shoppers in Korea are often advised to be wary of imitation gems (*mojo posok*), but copies (*mobang*) of famous brand products are more common than fake gems.

Mok (moke)—Some Korean imports and exports are often controlled by government-dispensed quotas (*mok*) based on the previous year's performance. This system has allowed individual companies to monopolize some import and export categories.

Mumohan (muu-moe-hahn)—Koreans are noted for their hospitality, which often verges on the extreme and stems from a compelling urge to both please and impress. This behavior gives the impression that they are unreasonably *mumohan*, or extravagant, by nature, often to their own detriment, but when others are conditioned to the same custom it all balances out.

Munan kanda (muun-ahn kahn-dah)—This is an institutionalized expression used to people of an equal or lower rank when inquiring about how things are going with them. It means "go and ask if someone is at peace" (because historically there were so many clan wars in Korea).

Munhwa (muun-whah)—Koreans are very proud of their *munhwa*, or culture, and this pride is an important part of their nationalism, their attitudes toward foreigners and their treatment of foreign businesspeople. Foreign visitors and residents in Korea are expected to exhibit suitable interest in the cultural accomplishments of the country, and to respect both cultural artifacts and laws that mandate a cultural component in many business decisions.

Myungmul (me-yung-muul)—Each of the major geographical areas in Korea has a certain number of *myungmul*, or famous products, for which it has been noted for centuries. The items are popular among Korean travelers from other areas as gifts and souvenirs.

Nat dungjang (naht duung-jahng)—Literally "day lamp," this term is a derogatory reference to people in companies—often managers and executives who do very little work and appear to make little or no contribution to their departments—much as lights left on during the day.

Noryon-ga (no-ree-own-gah)—Because of their long history of venerating scholarship and knowledge, Koreans have a great deal of respect for true experts (*noryon-ga*). This has proven to be a significant advantage to foreign professionals associated with Korean companies.

Ockji (oak-jee)—A familiar phrase in the Korean business lexicon, *ockji* means "I'll do it anyway" when one has been given a task that appears to be impossible.

Ondanghan (own-dahng-hahn)—The Korean concept of *ondanghan*, or fairness, often differs from the Western interpretation because it is not necessarily an absolute principle, and changes with circumstances. For example, Koreans believe it is unfair for the US to expect reciprocal access to its market, which is much smaller and more vulnerable than the American market.

Ondol (own-dole)—Sometime before the first century BC, Koreans developed a central radiant heating system to warm their homes and buildings during the cold winter months—more than 2,000 years before central heating was to become common anywhere else in the world. The system consisted of running pipes beneath the floors of buildings and forcing the heat from wood-burning stoves to circulate through the pipes. People sat and slept on mats on the warm floors. The *ondol* system of heating is still common in Korea. Modern multilevel apartments use water heated by furnaces.

Oryo u shijiman (oh-ree-yoe uu shejee-mahn)—Another institutional phrase that is used often in Korea, this means in essence, "I know it is difficult but please do your best (to do me a favor or help me get something done)."

Pangsongmang (pahng-song-mahng)—The nature of Korean society has resulted in the use of *pangsongmang*, or networks, as the primary form of mutual help and cooperation in both private matters and in business. The institutionalized networks include the extended family, school classmates, people born in the same village or town, and friends made while serving in the military or while working for the same government agencies or ministries.

Piso (pee-soe)—Foreign managers working in Korea are advised to hire their own private secretaries (*piso*)—as opposed to allowing a joint-venture partner or someone else to hire them—in order to ensure a greater degree of loyalty and obligation.

Poikotu (poy-kot-tuu)—Because of national and cultural cohesiveness, Koreans are often able to act together for popular causes in a way that is the envy of such poly-cultural countries as the US. One instance of this is boycotts (*poikotu*) against the products of countries that offend them. On other occasions, said one Korean business executive, "We simply order our wives and family not to buy certain products."

Ponggonjogin (pong-gahnjoe-gheen)—Many of the social and political tenets of Korea are still basically *ponggonjogin* (feudal), and often interfere with the attempts of the Koreans to adopt a democratic form of government and society. Feudalistic thinking plays a significant role in the management of many government offices and companies.

Ponosu (poe-no-suu)—The twice-a-year bonus (*ponosu*) has become an integral part of the income of company employees in Korea. Companies are often called on to pay bonuses even when profits do not warrant them. This is done to avoid disappointing and angering employees as well as to maintain the firm's public reputation.

Pop (pap)—Korean law (*pop*) is said to be much more like German law than American law, and is therefore difficult for Americans to understand and appreciate. There is also a strong tendency to interpret the law from both a Confucian and nationalistic bias.

Posu (poe-suu)—It is often said that Koreans work for bosses (*posu*) instead of companies (the opposite of the Japanese), because of the deep personal bonds that are essential for Koreans to maintain a successful relationship, whether privately or in business. As a result of this, Korean workers often display more loyalty to their immediate bosses than to their employers.

Puha (puu-hah)—The role of the *puha*, or follower, in Korean companies is of vital importance, especially when the chairman of the board or the president decides to step down. In most cases, company heads are regarded as "dynasties" in which the retiring leader has the right to name his successor, often his most faithful follower or the one whom he thinks is most likely to continue his philosophy and policies.

Puin (puu-een)—Another person's wife. Also, *ojumoni* (oh-juu-moe-nee).

Pumjil (pume-jeel)—With their long history as manufacturers of handicrafts which long ago achieved the *pumjil* (quality) of fine arts, Koreans have a cultural sense of and natural desire for both good design and quality in all of their products. These deeply entrenched traits were a major factor in their rapid emergence as an exporting nation.

Pyonhosa (pyone-hoe-sah)—There are few *pyonhosa* (attorneys) in Korea because the Korean concept of personal and business relations generally precludes their use in settling disputes or negotiating business or financial deals. Korean executives who were educated abroad are, of course, much more comfortable with the use of attorneys in their business dealings.

Pyong (p'yong)—One *pyong* is a specific measurement of 3.3 square meters, and is used to describe the size of plots of land, the floor space of buildings, etc. The number of *pyong* in a person's home or apartment is also a measure of his social status.

Rotori (roe-tah-ree)—This is the Korean pronunciation of rotary, which refers to a traffic circle. For some reason, there are many rotaries in Seoul, and until you get used to them, they can make driving in the city more confusing than usual.

Sang-min (sahng-meen)—The lower-middle class in feudal Korea (*sang-min*) was made up of artists, craftsmen, fishermen, farmers and merchants.

Sangpyo (sahng-pyoe)—Korean consumers are typically very *sangpyo*, or brand-conscious. Those who can afford it often prefer to buy famous international brands even when equivalent Korean-made products are available in the market.

Sasaenghwal (sah-sang-whal)—The concept of *sasaenghwal*, or privacy, is not nearly as explicit or as strong in Korea as it is in much of the West. Because of the communal nature of life during their long feudal period, Koreans could have few secrets from each other. When this was combined with the Confucian concept of suppressing individuality in the interest of the group, a desire for personal privacy was considered an aberration. The tendency for Korean employees to be unconcerned about keeping things private is often upsetting to foreign managers.

Seibei (say-bay)—At the beginning of the new business year, usually between January 3 and 5, it is customary for Korean businesspeople to make courtesy calls on the directors and presidents of their client or customer companies to bow and ask for their continued patronage during the new year. This is known as *seibei*, or "beginning of the year bow."

Seoncho haget sumnida (say-own-choe hah-gate sume-nee-dah)—"I will take care of it." This commonly used phrase, when translated into English, implies that whatever the problem or request, the individual making the statement intends to literally take care of it—to come through. In the original Korean, however, this meaning is not so explicit. It means something more like "I will do my best but I'm not making any promises"—which is a very common cop-out when you have no intention of doing anything at all.

Sahun (sah-huun)—Virtually all large Korean companies have their own *sahun*, or slogans and company precepts. Most of the slogans and statements represent the personal philosophies of the founders. In some Korean companies, these precepts are read aloud at morning meetings and on special occasions.

Sapyo (sah-pee-yoe)—It is rare for Korean employees to leave a large and well-known company. When they do, most write *sapyo*, or formal resignation letters, stating their reasons. If the employee is considered valuable by top management, considerable effort may be made to persuade him to remain with the company.

Seiryuk kwon (say-ree-yuke kwahn)—Literally, "power place," this term refers to a favored bar or cabaret which one frequents often, is well known by the management and staff, and therefore has "influence." Businesspeople like to take guests, especially foreign visitors, to their *seiryuk kwon* because they are assured of special service, and the guests are more likely to be impressed with these businesspeople.

Shigan-ul omsuhanun (she-ghan-ule ohm-suu-hahnuun)—Because of the strict military training most Korean men undergo and the pace of business in Korea, everyone tends to be very punctual (*shigan-ul omsuhanun*), and expects the same of others.

Shihom (she-home)—*Shihom*, or examinations, are a fact of life for young Koreans. Each educational step upward is marked by increasingly difficult examinations, with the most difficult being the one to enter a prestigious university. Finally, those seeking jobs with the more desirable commercial companies and government offices must also pass tough examinations that weed out all but the brightest.

Shijo (she-joe)—More so perhaps than in most countries, the *shijo* (founders) of Korean companies tend to mold them totally from top to bottom in the image of their own management as well as social philosophies. One of the first things one should find out about a Korean company is whether or not it is still headed by its founder, and if so, to obtain as deep an understanding as possible of his personal beliefs and policies.

Shikunbap (she-kuun-bahp)—"Cold food." When an individual in a company or a government office or agency is shunted off of the promotional ladder—an obvious sign that he is not going to reach the higher executive levels—he is sometimes described as being fed *shikunbap*, or cold food. Most such people lose much of their power or influence within the company since everyone knows they are not going to advance in the managerial hierarchy. Foreign businesspeople approaching Korean companies should try to make sure they have not been shuffled off onto a "cold food eater."

Shimushik (she-muu-sheek)—On the first day of business after the New Year holidays, Korean companies generally hold *shimushik*, or "starting business ceremonies," to mark the beginning of a new year. Executives and managers make short speeches in a festive atmosphere.

Shinyong (sheen-yong)—Interpersonal and business relations in Korea are based more on personal trust (*shinyong*) than on any code of ethics, philosophy or body of law. It is thus vital that foreign businesspeople establish strong personal bonds with their Korean agents or partners.

Shimalseo (she-mahl-say-oh)—A *shimalseo* is a letter of apology, often written following some kind of problem as an official expression of regret aimed at repairing damaged relations.

Soju (soejuu)—A liquor made from rye, sweet potatoes, and sometimes other grains, *soju* was introduced into Korea from Mongolia in the 14th century. It is a clear drink, resembling vodka, and although described as "mild" by Koreans, it has a kick like a mule.

Songbyul hoe (song-be-ule hay)—Such events as departing for overseas assignments are ceremoniously observed in Korean companies by *songbyul hoe*, or farewell parties, at which there are speeches and numerous toasts. The parties serve to strengthen personal ties among the employees and reinforce their attachment to the company.

Songgum (song-gume)—There are a variety of restrictions controlling the remittance of money (*songgum*) out of Korea. Generally speaking, the government prefers that no profits be exported from the country. It is therefore important that this facet of any joint venture be clearly approved in advance.

Songsaeng (song-sang)—*Songsaeng*, or teachers, have traditionally been highly respected in Korea, where education was so important in society. It is often applied to professionals outside of the teaching profession as a way of showing special respect. It is also sometimes used to butter up individuals for one purpose or another. The honorific *nim*, which is the equivalent of "mister," is often added to *songsaeng*.

Soryu (soe-r'yuu)—There is a contradiction in the use of *soryu* (documents) in Korea that is often bothersome and a detriment to business. Very few documents are created in the regular course of business. Most of the interaction between managers and personnel is verbal and few written records are kept. This often leads to misinterpretation and confusion that can be straightened out only by additional meetings. On the other hand, excessive documentation is typical of government offices, agencies and ministries, and is a special burden on businesspeople.

Sungshil (suung-sheel)—One of the most important words in the Korean businessperson's vocabulary, *sungshil* means "sincerity" or "integrity." It is the quality employers look for in new employees, and in general is regarded as more important than technical knowledge or skill. This is also the quality Korean businesspeople first look for in their foreign contacts. They feel that without this quality in a relationship, it is better not to do business with the individual or company concerned.

Tabang (tah-bahng)—Literally "tea rooms," these ubiquitous shops (there are some 35,000 of them in the country, with a quarter of these in Seoul) originally served only tea, but have evolved into the Korean equivalent of the coffee shop and serve a wide variety of drinks and food. They come in several kinds—those catering to businesspeople, to young dating couples, to the affluent "cafe-set" and to gourmet coffee lovers.

Taeguk (tay-gook)—The national flag of Korea. It consists of a circle of interlocking red and blue halves which represent the flow of the seasons, with the red or *yang* half representing the sun and the light, positive, masculine, active aspect of the cosmos, and the blue side representing the moon and the feminine, passive, cold, dark aspect of the cosmic forces.

Taeriin (tay-reen)—An agency (*taeriin*) is the easiest form of business relationship to establish in Korea, but there are a number of restrictions on the activities of agents of foreign firms that must be carefully weighed before deciding on this form of representation.

Taesa (tay-sah)—The position of *taesa*, or ambassador, to Korea is an interesting assignment that is also delicate and often frustrating because of cultural factors, including the Korean obsession-like pursuit of national economic goals. A veteran foreign ambassador in Seoul can be a valuable source of insight and information to an incoming company.

Taewu (tay-wuu)—This is a word that may be used on a card to mean something like "high rank" or "senior rank" without specifying a department or position. It is primarily used to describe the kind of service given to VIPs and special guests. Visiting businesspeople are often given this kind of treatment (and thereafter feel obligated to their hosts and inclined to be less demanding in their negotiations).

Tallyok (tahl-yoak)—There are two *tallyok* (calendars) used in Korea, the lunar calendar and the solar calendar. Holidays from both of the calendars are celebrated, so it is important for businesspeople to be familiar with both.

Tamye (tom-yay)—The Korean social etiquette that requires all favors and debts to be paid is known as *tamye*. It literally means "answering." This includes expressing thanks when appropriate, bowing, etc.

Tanshin buin (tahn-sheen buu-een)—This term refers to employees who are transferred from their original place of employment to a branch, subsidiary, or affiliated company—often in a distant city or even foreign country away from their families, forcing them to take care of themselves, like bachelors. The assignments are serious hardships for many older employees with families, but they are common because Korean companies systematically transfer personnel around throughout their organizations as part of their on-the-job training.

Tomping (tome-peeng)—This is "dumping," pronounced in Korean, in which the "d" sound and "t" sound are often interchangeable and indistinguishable. Koreans are perhaps more sensitive to charges of "dumping" (selling their goods in foreign markets at lower than production costs) than the Japanese because their overall export volume is much smaller and they regard such accusations as unfair, if not racially motivated.

Undaeng i (unn-dang ee)—The Korean word for the rear end, *undaeng i* is used in a number of compounds to describe specific types of people, from those who are slow or lazy to those who are a bit strange.

Yangban (yahng-bahn)—The upper class in feudal Korea, made up of scholar-bureaucrats (*munban*) and high ranking military officers (*mulban*). Many Koreans and foreign residents say the *yangban* social system still prevails, and now consists of high government bureaucrats, ranking military officers and newly rich businesspeople.

Yeui pomjol (yay-we pahm-jahl)—The precepts of Confucianism, in which the relationships between the sexes, the young and the old, and the different social classes are carefully and minutely prescribed, are still very strong in Korea, with the result that special attention should be given to appropriate *yeui pomjol*, or etiquette, in all personal and business relations. Generally speaking, Korean etiquette is based on respecting one's parents and elders, obeying superiors, avoiding comments or behavior that would hurt the other person's feelings or harm their "face," bowing at the right time and in the right manner, saying the right things at the right time, and following age-old customs in matters relating to life's main passages—coming of age, marriage, death, etc.

Yojung (yoe-juung)—This is what foreigners generally call a *kisaeng* house. *Kisaeng* actually means "hostess." *Yojung* means "inn," which in turn employs *kisaeng* to entertain its guests. *Kisaeng* are the equivalent of Japanese geisha—although some of them today are more like cabaret hostesses.

Yonhoe (yoan-hoe-eh)—Koreans are noted for their extravagant hospitality, especially when it comes to food. Dinners for foreign guests are almost always *yonhoe* (banquets), involving numerous courses, and a great deal of drinking.

Yuhaeng (yuu-hang)—Like their close Japanese neighbors, Koreans are very *yuhaeng* (fashion) conscious and concerned about being well dressed. This has helped fuel the development of a growing fashion industry in Korea.

Yuryuk ja (yuu-ree-yuke jah)—Literally, "a person with influence," meaning someone with sufficient power or clout to make things happen, especially in reference to matters concerning the government, or getting someone a job in a desirable government agency or company. Many companies owe much of their success to having a *yuryuk ja* on their side.

CHAPTER FIVE

Western Job Titles and Their Korean Equivalents

Management Titles

FOREIGN	KOREAN	TRANSLATION
Chairman	*Howe Jang*	Chairman of Board
President	*Sa Jang*	
Vice President	*Boo-Sa Jang*	
Managing Director	*Chunmoo Ee-Sa*	Principal Director
Director	*Sangmoo Ee-Sa*	Standing Director
General Manager	(No equivalent)	
Department Manager	*Boo Jang*	Department Chief
Assistant Dept Manager	*Cha Jang*	Vice Dept Chief
Section Manager	*Kwa Jang*	Section Chief
Assistant Section Mgr	*Daeri*	Branch Chief
Senior Clerk	*Joo Im Kye Won*	Principal Job, Branch Member

Factory Titles

FOREIGN	KOREAN	TRANSLATION
Factory Manager	*Kong Jang Jang*	Factory Chief
Department Manager	*Boo Jang*	Department Chief
Section Manager	*Kwa Jang*	Section Chief
Supervisor	*Daeri*	
	Branch Chief	
Foreman	*Joo Im*	Person in Charge

Other Titles

FOREIGN	KOREAN
Secretary	*Bee Seo*
Bookkeeper	*Kijangsuki*
Driver	*Oonjunsoo*
Typist	*Ta Jasoo*
Messenger	*Sa Hwan*

Department Names

FOREIGN	KOREAN
Accounting	*Howegae*
Engineering	Engineer
General Affairs	*Chong Mu*
Machine Shop	*Keekyea Kong*
Materials	*Chache*
Material Control	*Chache Kwanree*
Plant Maintenance	*Kong Jang Sisol Kwanree*
Production	*Saengsan*
Quality Control	*Pumcheel Kwanree*
Sales	*Panmae*
Shipping/Receiving	*Balsong/Sunap*

CHAPTER SIX

Guide to Korean Pronunciation

Pronunciation Guide to Vowels

A	Ya	O	Yo	O
Ah	Yah	Ah	Yah	Oh

Yo	U	Yu	U	I
Yoh	Uu	Yuu	Oi	Ee

Note that the third syllable in the top line (O) is pronounced more like an "a" than an "o". For example *oje* (yesterday) is pronounced ay-jay. *Odiso* (where) is pronounced ah-dee-soe. I have attempted to account for this factor in the phonetics following each word and sentence.

Pronunciation Guide to Multiple Vowels

Ae	Yae	E	Ye	Oe
Aeh	Yaeh	Eh	Yeh	Oeh

Wa	Wo	Wae	We	Wi
Wah	Wah	Wae	Weh	Wee

Pronunciation Guide for Syllables

Ka	Kya	Ko	Kyo	Ko
Kah	Kyah	Kah	Kyah	Koh

Kyo	Ku	Kyu	Ku	Ki
Kyoh	Kuu	Kyuu	Kuu	Kee

Na	**Nya**	**No**	**Nyo**	**No**
Nah	Nyah	Noo	Nyoe	No
Nyo	**Nu**	**Nyu**	**Nu**	**Ni**
Nyoh	Nuu	Nyuu	Nuu	Nee
Da	**Dya**	**Do**	**Dyo**	**Do**
Dah	Dyah	Doe	Dyoe	Doe
Dyo	**Du**	**Dyu**	**Du**	**Di**
Dyoe	Duu	Dyuu	Due	Dee
Ra	**Rya**	**Ro**	**Ryo**	**Ro**
Rah	Ryah	Roe	Ryoe	Roe
Ryo	**Ru**	**Ryu**	**Ru**	**Ri**
Ryoe	Ruu	Ryuu	Rue	Ree
Ma	**Mya**	**Mo**	**Myo**	**Mo**
Mah	Myah	Moe	Myoe	Moe
Myo	**Mu**	**Muu**	**Mu**	**Mi**
Myoe	Muu	Myuu	Mue	Me
Ba	**Bya**	**Bo**	**Byo**	**Bo**
Bah	Byah	Boe	Byoe	Boe
Byo	**Bu**	**Byu**	**Bu**	**Bi**
Byoe	Buu	Byuu	Bue	Bee
Sa	**Sya**	**So**	**Syo**	**So**
Sah	Syah	Soe	Syoe	Soe
Syo	**Su**	**Syu**	**Su**	**Si**
Syoe	Suu	Syuu	Sue	She
A	**Ya**	**O**	**Yo**	**O**
Ah	Yah	Ohh	Yeh	Oh

Yo	U	Yu	U	I
Yoe	Yuu	Yuu	Uu	Ee
Ja	**Jya**	**Yo**	**Jyo**	**Jo**
Jah	Jyah	Joe	Jyoe	Joe
Jyo	**Ju**	**Jyu**	**Ju**	**Ji**
Iyoe	Juu	Juu	Juu	Jee
Cha	**Chya**	**Cho**	**Chyo**	**Cho**
Chah	Chyah	Choe	Chyoe	Choe
Chyo	**Chu**	**Chyu**	**Chu**	**Chi**
Chyoe	Chuu	Chyuu	Chuu	Chee
Ka	**Kya**	**Ko**	**Kyo**	**Ko**
Kah	Kyah	Koe	Hyoe	Koe
Kyo	**Kuu**	**Kyu**	**Ku**	**Ki**
Kyoe	Kuu	Kyuu	Kuu	Kee
Ta	**Tya**	**To**	**Tyo**	**To**
Tah	Tyah	Toe	Tyoe	Toe
Tyo	**Tu**	**Tyu**	**Tu**	**Ti**
Tyoe	Tuu	Tyuu	Tue	Tee
Pa	**Pya**	**Po**	**Pyo**	**Po**
Pah	Pyah	Poe	Pyoe	Poe
Pyo	**Pu**	**Pyu**	**Pu**	**Pi**
Pyoe	Puu	Pyuu	Puu	Pee
Ha	**Hya**	**Ho**	**Hyo**	**Ho**
Hah	Hyah	Hoe	Hyoe	Hoe
Hyo	**Hu**	**Hyu**	**Hu**	**Hi**
Hyoe	Huu	Hyuu	Hue	Hee